John Brown's Raid

HARPERS FERRY AND THE COMING OF THE CIVIL WAR, OCTOBER 16–18, 1859

by Jon-Erik M. Gilot and Kevin R. Pawlak

EMERGING CIVIL WAR SERIES

Chris Mackowski, series editor
Cecily Nelson Zander, chief historian

The Emerging Civil War Series

offers compelling, easy-to-read overviews of some of the Civil War's most important battles and stories.

Recipient of the Army Historical Foundation's Lieutenant General Richard G. Trefry Award for contributions to the literature on the history of the U.S. Army

Also part of the Emerging Civil War Series:

Dreams of Victory: P. G. T. Beauregard in the Civil War
by Sean Michael Chick

Grant's Last Battle: The Story Behind the Personal Memoirs of Ulysses S. Grant
by Chris Mackowski

Hellmira: The Union's Most Infamous Civil War Prison Camp—Elmira, NY
by Derek Maxfield

The Last Days of Stonewall Jackson: The Mortal Wounding of the Confederacy's Greatest Icon
by Chris Mackowski and Kristopher D. White

Lincoln Comes to Gettysburg: The Creation of the Soldiers' National Cemetery and Lincoln's Gettysburg Address
by Bradley M. Gottfried and Linda I. Gottfried

Man of Fire: William Tecumseh Sherman in the Civil War
by Derek Maxfield

The Most Desperate Acts of Gallantry: George A. Custer in the Civil War
by Daniel T. Davis

Passing Through the Fire: Joshua Lawrence Chamberlain in the Civil War
by Brian F. Schwartz

To Hazard All: A Guide to the 1862 Maryland Campaign
by Rob Orrison and Kevin Pawlak

For a complete list of titles in the Emerging Civil War Series, visit www.emergingcivilwar.com.

John Brown's Raid

HARPERS FERRY AND THE COMING OF THE CIVIL WAR, OCTOBER 16–18, 1859

by Jon-Erik M. Gilot and Kevin R. Pawlak

EMERGING CIVIL WAR SERIES

Savas Beatie
California

First edition, first printing

ISBN-13 (paperback): 978-1-61121-597-7
ISBN-10 (ebook): 978-1-61121-598-4

Library of Congress Control Number: 2021056006

Names: Gilot, Jon-Erik M., author. | Pawlak, Kevin R., author.
Title: John Brown's Raid : Harpers Ferry and the coming of the Civil War, October 16–18, 1859 / by Jon-Erik M. Gilot and Kevin R. Pawlak.
Description: El Dorado Hills, CA : Savas Beatie, [2023] | Series: Emerging Civil War series | Includes bibliographical references and index. |
Summary: "The first shot of the American Civil War was not fired on April 12, 1861, in Charleston, South Carolina, but instead came on October 16, 1859, in Harpers Ferry, Virginia-or so claimed former-slave-turned-abolitionist Frederick Douglass. John Brown, the infamous fighter on the Kansas plains and detester of slavery, led a band of nineteen men on a desperate nighttime raid that targeted the Federal arsenal at Harpers Ferry. There, they planned to begin a war to end slavery in the United States"-- Provided by publisher.
Identifiers: LCCN 2021056006 | ISBN 9781611215977 (paperback) | ISBN 9781611215984 (ebook)
Subjects: LCSH: Harpers Ferry (W. Va.)--History--John Brown's Raid, 1859.
Classification: LCC F249.H2 G595 2022 | DDC 973.7/116092--dc23
LC record available at https://lccn.loc.gov/2021056006

Published by
Savas Beatie LLC
989 Governor Drive, Suite 102
El Dorado Hills, California 95762
Phone: 916-941-6896
sales@savasbeatie.com
www.savasbeatie.com

Savas Beatie titles are available at special discounts for bulk purchases in the United States by corporations, institutions, and other organizations. For more details, you may e-mail us at sales@savasbeatie.com or visit our website at www.savasbeatie.com for additional information.

Kevin:
To my parents,
Jerome & Teresa

Jon-Erik:
To my mother,
who first took me to Harpers Ferry as a child

and

To my wife,
who never declines an opportunity to go back there

Table of Contents

Footnotes for this volume are available at
https://emergingcivilwar.com/publication/footnotes/

List of Maps

Maps by Edward Alexander

PHOTO CREDITS: Jon-Erik Gilot (jeg); Kevin Pawlak (kp); George Best (gb); Frank Leslie's Illustrated Newspaper (flin); *Harper's Weekly* (hw); Library Company of Philadelphia (lcp); Library of Congress (loc); Linda Cunningham Fluharty Collection (lcf); Chris Mackowski (cm); Jessica Maxfield (jm); National Park Service (nps); National Portrait Gallery (npg); New York Public Library (nypl); New York State Archives (nysa); West Virginia Archives & History (wvah); West Virginia State Archives (wvsa); Wikimedia (w)

For the Emerging Civil War Series

Theodore P. Savas, *publisher*
Chris Mackowski, *series editor and co-founder*
Cecily Nelson Zander, *chief historian*
Sarah Keeney, *editorial consultant*

Maps by Edward Alexander
Design and layout by Jessica Maxfield

Acknowledgments

This book would not be possible without the continued support of many people.

No Emerging Civil War Series book is possible without Chris Mackowski, whom we thank for inspiring us not just to tell the story of battles but that of human beings. Ted Savas and his team at Savas Beatie make the process of publishing a book easier than it appears. Ed Alexander's excellent and original maps add a useful visual layer to John Brown's Raid.

Along the way, many eyes pored over our work and each reader made it a better book. Dennis Frye not only provided the book's foreword but read our original draft. Leon Reed and Emerging Civil War's Chris Kolakowski likewise reviewed our work and offered helpful comments. Friend and Civil War Trails Executive Director Drew Gruber ensured our tours were up to date with the most recent additions to Civil War Trails' signage. Any remaining faults with the work lie solely with us. Thanks to our editors, there are many fewer flaws.

Kevin:

First, I want to thank my co-author Jon-Erik. He eagerly jumped into this project and made it better. His knowledge of the John Brown story is first rate. I learned a lot from him and he was a pleasure to work with. Few know the craft of history and storytelling better than he.

A Civil War Trails sign stands near the Charles Town court house. (kp)

My journey with John Brown began in 2012, when Melinda Day and John King, supervisory rangers at Harpers Ferry National Historical Park, gave me my start in the field of history. From 2012 to 2014, I had the pleasure of working alongside a great group of historians, with each of whom I spent time discussing the story of John Brown's Raid. Those informal chats prepared me to write this book.

As always, my good friends George Best, Mike Galloway, Billy Griffith, Rob Orrison, and Dan Welch provided useful help along the way, whether it involved aiding us in the process of publishing the book or debating all things John Brown.

Lastly, I dedicate this book to my parents, Jerome and Teresa. They encouraged me to leave home and start a career and life for myself. Without their support, none of what I have accomplished thus far in life would be possible.

Jon-Erik:
The bulk of this book was written during the COVID-19 quarantine of 2020. As I sat at home for nearly three months I would often wake early and do some writing before my children were up. I would feel good about myself if I was at my desk and writing by 6:00 a.m. That sense of accomplishment only lasted until I realized that Kevin had been up writing since 4:00 am. His work ethic and positive attitude are simply unmatched. As a historian, he is second to none and I am thrilled to have had the opportunity to

work with him. Kevin—thank you for letting me share this journey with you.

Thanks to Emerging Civil War colleagues Phil Greenwalt, Rob Orrison, and Dan Welch for serving as sounding boards and offering suggestions as I navigated the process of writing my first book. Thanks to Adam Ochs Fleischer and Linda Cunningham Fluharty for sharing material from their personal collections, and Aaron Parsons and Joe Geiger for sharing photos from West Virginia Archives & History. Thanks also to Sean Duffy and Margaret Brennan, whose work continues to inspire me to find the personal stories within the larger narrative. Sean graciously edited my early drafts, only asking that I share a few socially-distant porch beers in return.

Thanks to my mother, grandmother, and late grandfather for introducing me to history and constantly encouraging my studies and writing. I had the good fortune to grow up in a small, historic village, but so did a lot of other kids. It was those early books and battlefield visits that truly defined who I was and who I would become. Without your unwavering support—and without that first trip to Harpers Ferry in 1997, mom—none of this would have been possible. Thank you for always believing in me.

Finally, thank you to my wife, my in-laws, Jeff and Donna, and my two beautiful daughters. Through the early mornings, late nights, and near constant extolling of John Brown, you graciously listened and encouraged me. Where colleagues challenge me to be a better historian, you challenge me to be a better husband, father, and man. Heather, thank you for agreeing to that first trip to Harpers Ferry, and for saying yes when we got there and I asked you to marry me. I selfishly wanted you to feel some connection there, and that perhaps one day you would want to return. Between the proposal,   this book, and the many trips in between, I hope I succeeded.

I firmly believe in the power of place—that our surroundings help shape who we are; what we know; how we remember. In all my travels I have never experienced a place more powerful than Harpers Ferry, and I feel a stronger connection with each passing visit. I challenge you, the reader, to go there and find your own story.

A monument at Harpers Ferry marks the original location of John Brown's Fort, which has been relocated but is still visible in the middle distance. (cm)

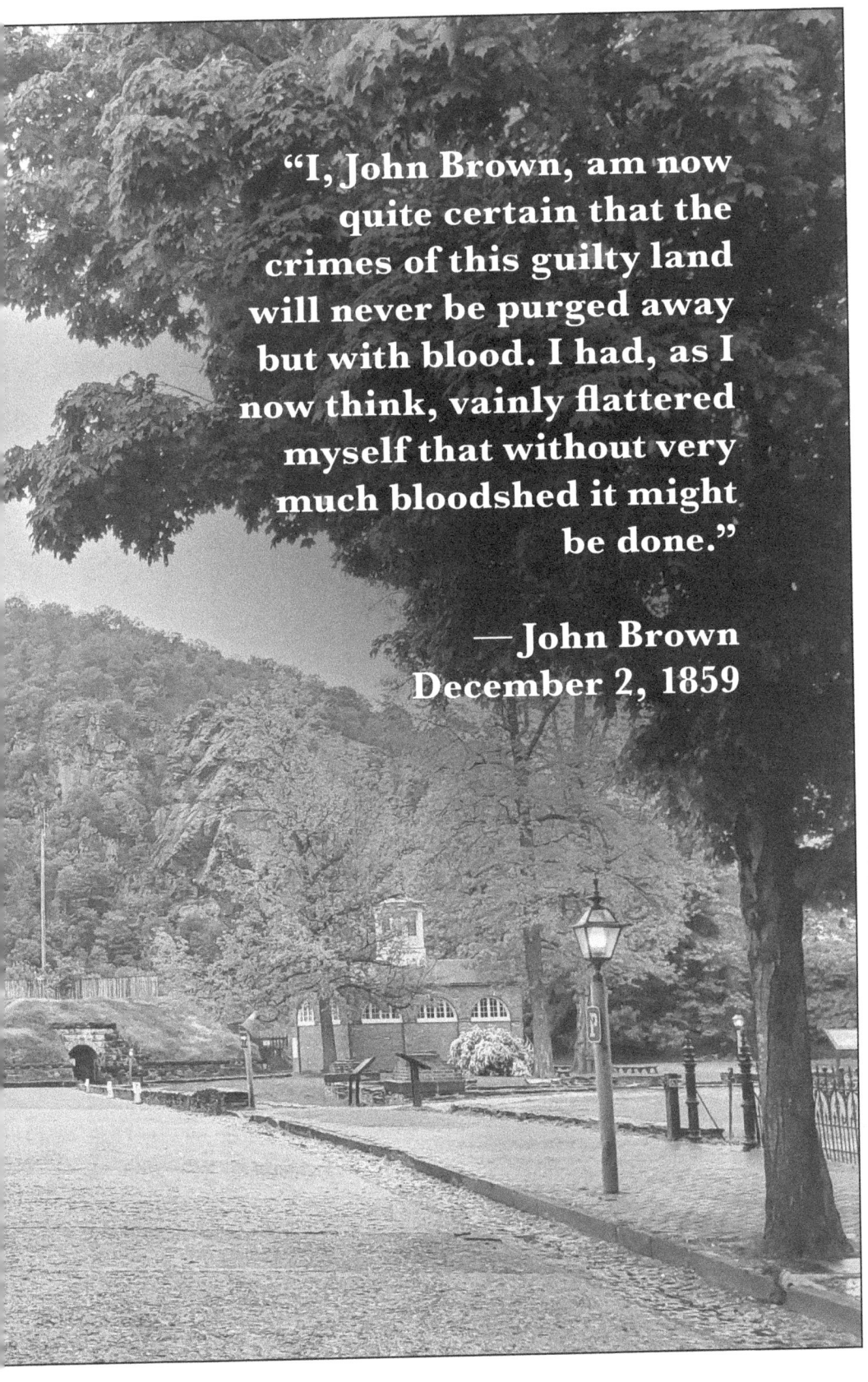

"I, John Brown, am now quite certain that the crimes of this guilty land will never be purged away but with blood. I had, as I now think, vainly flattered myself that without very much bloodshed it might be done."

— John Brown
December 2, 1859

Foreword

BY DENNIS E. FRYE

I stood on the porch of the log cabin, staring into darkness. Only the dim light of a candle lantern pierced the blackness.

Beside me was John Brown's great-great-great granddaughter.

The Kennedy farmhouse dripped in a light rain, just as it did 150 years before at that exact moment. The clock ticked toward 8 p.m. It was October 16th. *Not 1859.* No—the year 2009. We had gathered to commemorate the launch. The date and time coincided with a transformative moment in American history: Brown's commencement of his ultimate war to eradicate slavery.

Two hundred ticket holders gathered before us, squinting to discern our shadows prancing on the second-story porch. They peered at the lone light dangling from my arm. No lights emanated from the audience. No voices either. All respected the specialness, the reverence, of the place. All understood its portent. Each person knew. Each would be marching with John Brown.

I moved my lantern to portray the descendant of Annie Brown. We stood transfixed. We were witnessing a thread through time. She began reading recollections. Every word froze us; then moved us, transcending time. Annie, you see, lived with her father at the cabin. She helped hide his identity and guard his secrets as a lookout as John Brown gathered warriors and weapons beneath Elk Ridge in Washington County, Maryland. Ironic, was it not: Brown's revolution to terminate slavery would

After moving three times, John Brown's Fort was returned to the Lower Town at Harpers Ferry in 1968. (jm)

The Shenandoah and Potomac Rivers meet at Harpers Ferry. (jm)

Annie Brown was the last survivor of the Kennedy farmhouse occupants when she died in 1926. She spent the remainder of her life as a fierce defender of her father's legacy and memory. (loc)

commence in the first county in the United States named in honor of the Revolutionary hero.

After Annie's aura, I raised the lantern to light my face. Precisely 8 o'clock, it was, just as history recorded. I summoned my voice and spoke John Brown's final order from his headquarters: "Men, get on your arms. We shall proceed to the Ferry."

That night I dressed in 19th-century garb, and was armed—shepherding a Sharps Rifle. I plunged into the shadowy crowd, searching for my one horse and one wagon, the lone conveyance that had accompanied Brown that dreary night. I found my transporters along the Harpers Ferry Road, about 200 feet distant from the cabin's front porch. Holding my lantern in one hand and my rifle in the other, I motioned for the throng to join me. We were going to walk, through the darkness, five miles south to Harpers Ferry—in the footsteps of John Brown.

I muttered to myself, "Oh, my, what Brown may have accomplished with an army of 200." Our force was ten times the original.

We had arranged with the sheriff to shut off the road, offering us an avenue without modern intrusion. The Harpers Ferry Road had changed little since 1859, with hills and turns and slopes and winds seemingly ad infinitum in a lightless tunnel. I asked the crowd to speak not; not a word to spouse or sibling or child or friend. Their words, instead, should be heard only by themselves, within their souls. They were now marching with John Brown's soul.

Only the horse's hoofs and the creaking wheels of the wagon disrupted the silence. We progressed slowly, a phantom army and an army of phantoms. The incessant rain darkened the darkness, making it impossible to see the front of the column from the rear. No one spoke. No one cowered. No one dared to disrupt destiny.

An eerie glow beckoned us whence we reached the Potomac. We had descended a deep ravine, arriving at the river with sudden surprise. Downstream, we could see light. Down river one mile, we witnessed our target: Harpers Ferry.

Here we paused. When all gathered on the C & O Canal towpath, I probed with a few questions:

Do you realize you may never again see your loved ones?
Do you understand you are about to attack your own country?
Do you accept that you may die for this cause?

I asked for no answers—not aloud. Fate, quietly and respectfully, each person contemplated.

We continued downstream, our phalanx stretching astride the river's rapids. The glow grew brighter on the opposite bank, and in the shadows, we could see the bridge.

"Halt!"

We lurched. We stopped. Apparitions swarmed out of the fog. John Brown's soldiers offered us escort.

We climbed onto the railroad bridge and commenced our final trek. Midway across the river, I huddled the marchers. I asked us to stand silently, listening to the chorus of the Potomac and Shenandoah, their song echoing off the vertical cliffs of the Blue Ridge. I invited us to gaze, just yards downstream, at the stone pier ruins barely visible— the original bridge that brought Brown into Harpers Ferry. I asked us to ponder freedom, and the dignity of human life. I reserved this philosophical query for last. For once we stepped upon soil, in but a few more steps, neither freedom nor dignity existed for the enslaved.

John Brown's Fort greeted us. Alight with candles and reflections, its windows cast a gentle yellowish rainbow between its brick walls, reminding us of the ending of a severe storm. Here we paused, then passed, dumbfounded by its closed doors. Instead, we proceeded to the Arsenal—our target all along. Flaming torches then appeared. Engulfed, we seemed, in a firestorm. We hurriedly returned to The Fort. Here we felt safe.

But we were not.

The massive doors slowly opened, their wrought-iron hinges creaking, as if weeping. A man, in 19th century apparel, emerged. He stared at us, bewildered; then announced his name. But his name was not his. Another followed, then another. Twenty-one in all. Each of John Brown's soldiers. After each name, we heard one descriptor: "killed"; "hanged"; "escaped."

We stood there. Watching. . . Listening . . . Witnessing. . . .

We understood. Their souls, connecting with our souls, and John Brown's soul—marching on.

We had experienced the ultimate interaction with history—*power of place.*

This book will take you to these places.

There, you will discover, and experience, their power.

John Brown's Fort
as it stands today. (jm)

$\mathcal{P}rologue$

> "I think the lesson of the hour is insurrection. Insurrection of thought always precedes the insurrection of arms. The last twenty years have been an insurrection of thought. We seem to be entering on a new phase of this great American struggle..."
> — Wendell Phillips, *November 1, 1859*

John Brown's Raid on Harpers Ferry is widely acknowledged as a cataclysmic event that catapulted the United States towards civil war—"The meteor of the war," opined poet Herman Melville. Brown was vilified in the south, lionized in the north; his strike at slavery forced people to choose sides on the long-simmering issue. One modern biographer notes that Brown "reduced the margin for neutrality or moderation on the slavery question, pushing everyone on both sides of the issue towards the extremes."

However, the raid at Harpers Ferry was only the latest in more than a century of violence and insurrections relating to slavery. Notable among these were the Stono Rebellion of 1739 and German Coast Uprising of 1811, where over the course of two days

LEFT: **A larger-than-life painting of John Brown greets visitors at the John Brown Museum in Harpers Ferry. The original, *Tragic Prelude*, was painted by John Steuart Curry for the Kansas State Capitol. This "crazy prophet" image of Brown has become one of the most recognizable images of him.** (cm)

RIGHT: **Memories of Nat Turner's 1831 Rebellion stoked southern fears of slave uprisings.** (loc)

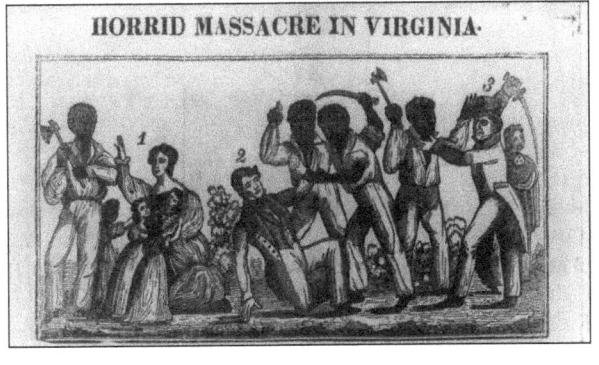

hundreds of slaves burned plantations and crops over a twenty-mile swath near New Orleans. Twenty years later Nat Turner's Rebellion in Southampton, Virginia, resulted in the deaths of more than 170 whites and African Americans, while maritime insurrections aboard the *Amistad* (1839) and *Creole* (1841) splashed across newspapers. (Frederick Douglass even penned a short story on the *Creole* case.) Violence in Christiana, Pennsylvania (1851), and Oberlin, Ohio (1858), relating to the 1850 Fugitive Slave Law, portended a rising concern in the south that both slaves and abolitionists were growing emboldened to override the law of the land. Abolitionist Gerrit Smith opined the necessity of such insurrections as "a terrible remedy for a terrible wrong," while abolitionist preacher Henry Highland Garnet implored slaves to revolt. In what would become known as the "Call to Rebellion" speech, Garnet called on slaves to "strike for your liberties . . . rather die freemen than live to be slaves." The *Charleston Mercury* warned that "Developments are rapidly showing that a wide-scheme was maturing [in] the North for insurrections throughout the South. The South must control her own destinies or perish."

During the Christiana Riot of September 11, 1851, free Blacks, escaped slaves, and white men resisted and killed a slavecatcher attempting to apprehend slaves in Pennsylvania through the Fugitive Slave Act. (lcp)

Beginning in 1854 and continuing for more than six years, anti-slavery and pro-slavery forces fought a civil war along the Missouri-Kansas border—a conflict hallmarked by violence, bloodshed, and guerrilla warfare—to determine the balance of power between slave states and free. The fighting was so severe that it came to be known as "Bleeding Kansas." The Kansas-

Nebraska Act—the brainchild of Democratic senator Stephen A. Douglas—was an attempt at continued compromise through popular sovereignty, wherein residents of the territory would vote on whether to be admitted as a slave or free state. Proponents of both factions, including John Brown and his family, flooded Kansas to swing the vote in their favor. However, the violence between the so-called Jayhawkers (anti-slavery "free-soilers") and Border Ruffians (pro-slavery) that

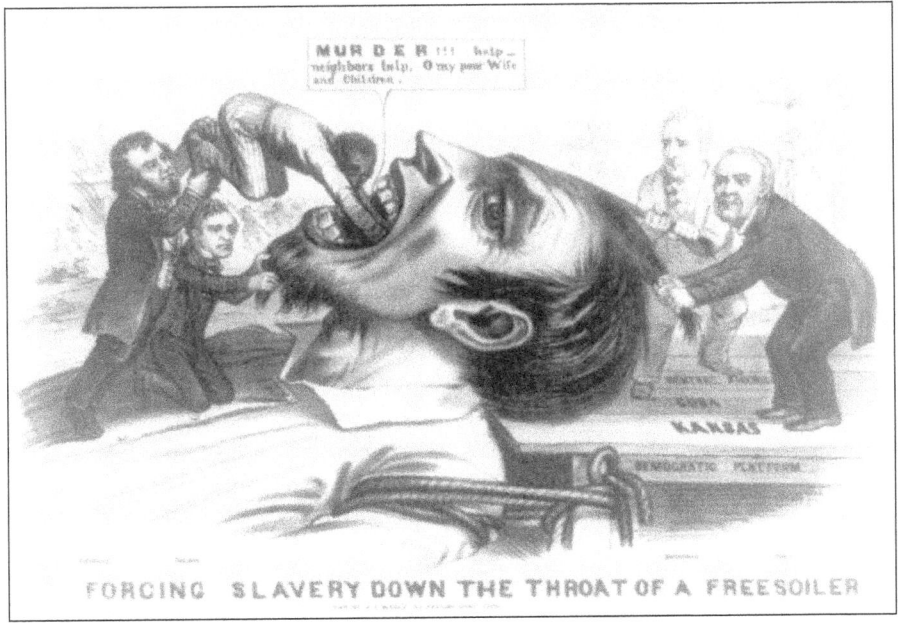

FORCING SLAVERY DOWN THE THROAT OF A FREESOILER

engulfed Kansas during this period seemed distant, even unconcerning, to much of the country. Indeed, one southern newspaper editor remarked, "why would we expend our blood and treasure on an issue where our immediate interests are not concerned?"

Nowhere was the violence of Bleeding Kansas more pronounced than at Pottawatomie Creek, where in May 1856, John Brown directed the murder of five pro-slavery men. Brown earned widespread notoriety, the murders ushering in the deadliest period of the conflict, in which 29 people were killed in the three months following the murders at Pottawatomie, or nearly four times the number killed during the previous two years.

From October 16–18, 1859, at Harpers Ferry, John Brown brought that violence, that fight over slavery, from the plains of Kansas to Virginia's Shenandoah Valley. Governor Henry Wise attributed Brown's actions to his having learned "the skill of the

The Bleeding Kansas conflict was fought in the press, the politics, and in the new territory itself. This cartoon pictures Democrats, including future president James Buchanan, "shoving slavery down the throat" of an anti-slavery man. (loc)

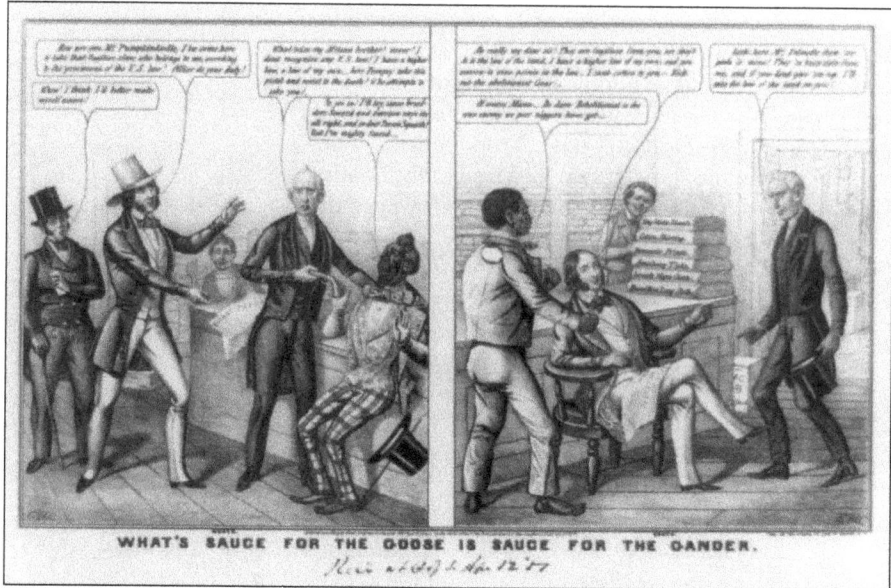

WHAT'S SAUCE FOR THE GOOSE IS SAUCE FOR THE GANDER.

In this 1851 cartoon satirizing the Fugitive Slave Act, the *Charleston Mercury* depicts an abolitionist offering a pistol to a slave, telling him to "resist to the death." (loc)

Henry Highland Garnet was a prominent abolitionist and himself a former slave. He became the first African American to address the halls of Congress on February 12, 1865, to mark the passage of the Thirteenth Amendment. (npg)

Indian in savage warfare" from his time in Kansas, using this lesson against "the oldest and largest slaveholding state to surprise one of its strongest holds." In response to Wendell Phillips's soliloquy on insurrection, Wise urged Virginians to "organize and arm . . . let us defend our own position, or yield it at once. Let us have action and not resolves: definitive settlement . . . no more temporizing the constitution, and no more compromise." Brown's far-reaching ties to prominent abolitionists throughout the North further stoked fears of invading abolitionist armies and contributed to a rise in militarism throughout the South in the months following the raid, particularly in the border states. Virginia, for instance, increased militia spending by more than $500,000 in the year following John Brown's Raid.

And yet the events at Harpers Ferry did not qualify as an insurrection any more in 1859 than they do today. Brown's own writings and interviews dispute the claim. When fiery Congressman Clement Vallandigham questioned whether Brown had anticipated a general uprising of the slaves, Brown emphatically stated he did not, nor did he wish it. Brown instead "expected to gather them up from time to time, and set them free," leveraging the mountainous terrain to hide his men and exchanging hostages for slaves. Brown anticipated such "lightning strikes" would destabilize the economy of the slave market in the Upper South, rendering the area too much of a risk to slaveholders.

In staging this economic warfare, Brown hoped to avert the bloodshed of earlier anti-slavery violence, vowing only to fight in self-defense.

Yet violence did swirl at Harpers Ferry, claiming the lives of innocent civilians, including two African Americans, one enslaved, the other free. The die for war was cast. Fire-eating secessionist Edmund Ruffin was elated at the news, believing the raid to be just what was needed to "stir the sluggish blood of the south." The "irrepressible conflict" that William Henry Seward prophesied only one year earlier was now a reality. Brown himself believed the nation had reached the tipping point, prophetically warning that "You had better—all you people of the South—prepare yourselves for a settlement of that question that must come up for settlement sooner than you are prepared for . . . you may dispose of me very easily. I am nearly disposed of now. But this question is still to be settled—this negro question, I mean—the end of that is not yet."

A retrospective Frederick Douglass perhaps said it best while visiting Harpers Ferry in 1881: "If John Brown did not end the war that ended slavery, he did at least begin the war that ended slavery."

While Brown had hoped to fight only in self-defense in his mission to liberate the slaves, his plans quickly went awry at Harpers Ferry. (loc)

The 23-acre John Brown
Memorial Park in Osawatomie,
Kansas, includes the John
Brown Museum State
Historic Site. (loc)

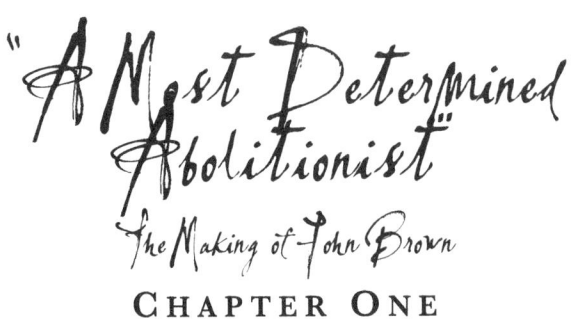

"A Most Determined Abolitionist"

The Making of John Brown

CHAPTER ONE

MAY 1800 - OCTOBER 1856

For a man whose name was destined to splash across newspapers around the world, a man who scores of monographs have attempted to explain and dissect, and a man who today remains as polarizing a figure as he was more than 160 years ago, John Brown came from the most inauspicious of beginnings. Born on May 9, 1800, to devout Calvinist parents in Torrington, Connecticut, Brown's formative years were dominated by the family's rigid religious principles, imbuing in him what some scholars have explained away as religious fanaticism. Rather than a fanatic or prophet, Brown viewed himself as "an instrument in the hands of Providence," particularly regarding the plight of the slave.

Slavery was in fact older than the nation itself, the first slaves arriving in Virginia in 1619. However, with the banning of the international slave trade in 1808, many felt that slavery would die of natural causes. Instead, Eli Whitney's cotton gin and the resulting explosion in cotton production in the southern states ensured a

John Brown's birthplace in Torrington, Connecticut. The house was destroyed by fire in 1918. (wvsa)

longstanding need for slave labor. By the eve of the Civil War, the nation counted nearly four million slaves, more than any other time since the formation of the United States, with Virginia itself accounting for nearly 500,000. An increase in abolitionists—those calling for slavery's abolition, and those willing to fight to see its end—accompanied the explosion in the slave

John Brown built this tannery near Meadville, Pennsylvania, in 1825. Like his boyhood home, the tannery was destroyed by fire in 1907. Today the site is seasonally open to visitors. (wvsa)

population. Standing among such early abolitionist luminaries as Charles Osborn and Benjamin Lundy was John Brown's own father, Owen Brown.

The elder Brown removed his family to Hudson on the Ohio frontier in 1805, where young John's formal education ended as he went to work in his father's tannery. Owen Brown was himself an outspoken activist in the Ohio anti-slavery community. From Hudson, the elder Brown founded the Western Reserve Anti-slavery Society as well as the Free Congregational Church, a congregation devoted to anti-slavery activism. Owen Brown likewise worked with the Ohio Anti-Slavery Society, to whom he railed in 1837 of the need for better education for the state's African American children. To this end, Brown served as a trustee at Oberlin College, one of the first colleges in the country to admit African Americans and women.

During the War of 1812, Owen Brown secured contracts to provide cattle to army outposts. Brown tasked his young son, John, to drive herds to camps sometimes more than 100 miles distant from his home. It was on one such trip that young Brown first witnessed the horrors of slavery. As Brown later recalled, he saw a slave nearly his own age "badly clothed, poorly fed & lodged in cold weather & beaten before his eyes with Iron Shovels or any other thing that came first to hand." This singular event, paired with his father's anti-slavery influences, galvanized John Brown into a "most determined Abolitionist" and to "declare, or Swear: Eternal war with Slavery."

As a teenager Brown struck out on his own, beginning a string of what have become highly

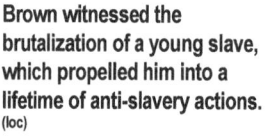

Brown witnessed the brutalization of a young slave, which propelled him into a lifetime of anti-slavery actions. (loc)

publicized failed business interests. Following a short stint in divinity school, Brown took the trade imparted from his father and opened a tannery business. He later relocated the business to western Pennsylvania, remaining there for nearly a decade before returning to Ohio in 1836. There Brown dabbled in land speculation and livestock sales. Mounting debts and the financial downtown of the 1830s rendered Brown insolvent, resulting in his bankruptcy in 1842. The following year he ventured into sheep herding and wool-growing. While he gained acclaim as a breeder and purveyor of sheep, this venture likewise ended in failure. While it is easy to dismiss John Brown as a poor businessman, his losses and financial difficulties are more emblematic of a time of volatile economic

Outspoken abolitionist and journalist Elijah P. Lovejoy was killed by a pro-slavery mob in November 1837 at Alton, Illinois, and his printing press was dumped into the Mississippi River. A portion of the press was discovered in 1915 and is today on display at the office of the *Alton Telegraph*. (nypl)

uncertainty, far different from the security today entrusted to both lenders and borrowers. Meanwhile, Brown continued to grow his family, fathering seven children with his first wife, Dianthe Lusk, who Brown married in 1820 and who died in 1832, and another thirteen children with his second wife, Mary Ann Day, who he married in 1833. Nine of Brown's offspring died in childhood.

While facing continued reverses in his businesses and his financial status, Brown continued to remain involved in anti-slavery activities. In an 1834 letter to his brother Frederick, Brown wrote that he had "been trying to devise some means whereby I might do something in a practical way for my poor fellow-men who are in bondage," even proposing to acquire a young slave boy to raise and educate within the Brown family. Following the 1837 Alton, Illinois, murder of outspoken abolitionist and printer Elijah P. Lovejoy by a pro-slavery mob, Brown rose from his seat during a prayer meeting at Hudson, Ohio, and exclaimed, "Here, before God, in the presence of these witnesses,

In this, the earliest known photograph of John Brown (ca. 1846-1847), Brown is holding a flag emblazoned with the words "Subterranean Pass Way," or the 'highway' envisioned by Brown for transporting slaves north to freedom. (npg)

from this time, I consecrate my life to the destruction of slavery." John Brown Jr. later recalled that in 1839, his father informed the family of his intention to defeat slavery "by force and arms." Brown's family thus became the first enlistees in this war against slavery, with Brown invoking the gospel and entreating them to "break the jaws of the wicked and pluck the spoil out of his teeth."

Brown's anti-slavery views became more pronounced between 1846 and 1849 while he was living in Springfield, Massachusetts, and pursuing the wool-trading business. Here, Brown hired African American employees and worshipped with them at the local Zion Methodist Church. It was also in

Springfield that Brown made the acquaintance of abolitionist luminaries, including Frederick Douglass. Brown and Douglass first met in February 1848. Douglass later recalled that meeting Brown was "the most interesting part of my visit to Springfield," and that Brown shook his hand "with a grip peculiar to anti-slavery men." Brown's very soul, Douglass felt, "had been pierced with the iron of slavery."

Brown confided in Douglass his plan for freeing the slaves—"lightning raids" along the Allegheny Mountains, whose natural barriers could hide an army of insurgents while shuttling slaves north to freedom. Rather than murder or maim slaveholders, Brown instead argued to "destroy the money value of slave property" by "rendering such property insecure." Brown proposed starting with some 25 men, armed and equipped, who would "induce the slaves to join them," despite efforts to stop them. Douglass argued that Brown would be hunted, surrounded, and very likely killed, yet Brown was unfazed, telling Douglass "he had no better use for his life than to lay it down in the cause of the slave."

The following year Brown moved his family north to the Adirondack Mountains. From their North Elba, New York, homestead, the Brown clan worked with the neighboring community of Timbucto, an African American colony that had been established by philanthropist and abolitionist (and later co-conspirator of the Harpers Ferry Raid) Gerrit Smith. Brown assisted the colonists in surveying land, planting crops, and farm work, and became fast friends with the local African American population. Simultaneously, Brown attempted to divest his wool business and traveled as far as London to sell his remaining stock. However, developments in the United States Congress, which threatened the safety and security of Brown's new friends, drew his attention back towards the evils of slavery.

Pushing the United States ever further westward, the Manifest Destiny movement of the 1840s ensured that slavery would remain a contentious political issue. The 1820 Missouri Compromise established slavery's line of demarcation (the 36°30' parallel) and sought to establish a balance of power between slave states and free. However, the addition of California to the Union threatened to upset this delicate balance. While the Compromise of 1850 admitted California as a free state, it left open the question of slavery in the New

Frederick Douglass escaped from slavery in 1838 and become a leading voice in the abolitionist movement. Douglass was impressed by Brown and remained an acquaintance for the remainder of Brown's life. Although he eventually opted not to join John Brown's Raid, he believed that "With the Allegheny Mountains for his pulpit, the country for his church and the whole civilized world for his audience," Brown "was a thousand times more effective as a preacher than as a warrior." (npg)

The Fugitive Slave Act, nicknamed as the "Bloodhound Bill," was one of the most divisive issues in the decade prior to the Civil War. (loc)

Estimates range as high as 100,000 slaves who escaped bondage via the Underground Railroad. (nypl)

FUGITIVE SLAVE AS ADVERTISED FOR CAPTURE

Mexico and Utah territories. More concerning to John Brown and the millions of African Americans in the United States—both free and enslaved—was the 1850 passage of the Fugitive Slave Act, which allowed for the arrest of alleged escaped slaves anywhere in the country and their return into slavery without the benefit of a trial by jury. The Fugitive Slave Act also levied fines and imprisonment on anyone harboring or assisting an escaped slave. This legislation brought the fight over slavery from the halls of Congress to the hearthstones of America, north and south.

John Brown envisioned the Fugitive Slave Act as "the means of making more Abolitionists than all the lectures we have had for years" and encouraged his African-American compatriots to "trust in God, and keep their powder dry." While back in Springfield in January 1851, Brown organized the United States League of Gileadites, an organization aimed at protecting the city's African American community from the Fugitive Slave Act. In the League's charter, Brown implored that members "Hold on to your weapons, and never be persuaded to leave them. Stand by one another and by your friends while a drop of blood remains; and be hanged, if you must..." While his hopes of the League spreading to other cities did not materialize, no slaves are known to have been apprehended from Springfield under the Fugitive Slave Act. Brown tested this devotion to his own charter just eight years later at Harpers Ferry.

Brown removed his family back to Ohio in 1851 to settle debts accumulated by his wool business but planned to return his family to North Elba, leaving a daughter there who had married Brown's future Bleeding Kansas compatriot Henry Thompson. Back in Ohio, the Browns were active in shuttling fugitive slaves northward as far as Detroit. Brown at last dissolved his wool business interests in early 1854 and hoped to return his family to their North Elba farmstead. Events in Kansas instead drew the Brown family westward.

In the spring of 1854, Congress passed the Kansas-Nebraska Act, opening the territories to

settlers willing to travel west and tame the expansive lands. Rather than abiding by earlier compromises over the issue of slavery, the bill instead allowed for "Popular Sovereignty," which allowed residents of the territory to decide whether to permit slavery within its boundaries. Pro-slavery factions essentially ceded the Nebraska territory to anti-slavery settlers. Kansas, however, situated west of slaveholding Missouri, became a battleground for the fight over slavery and a precursor to the bloodshed that would be even more widespread in the coming civil war. Both sides prepared for the fight.

Brown viewed the mountainous area of northern Virginia, western Maryland, and south-central Pennsylvania as an ideal area from which to launch his "lightning raids" against slavery. (loc)

As pro-slavery settlers flooded west across the Missouri border, wealthy philanthropists and abolitionists in the north sponsored emigration to the Kansas territory. The New England Emigrant Aid Society shuttled settlers west and established the town of Lawrence astride the Kansas River. Lawrence soon became the flashpoint of the Kansas conflict that gave the territory the name "Bleeding Kansas." Senator William H. Seward, a vocal opponent of the Kansas-Nebraska Act, goaded pro-slavery men from the floor of the Senate: "Come on, then, gentlemen of the slave states; since there is no escaping your challenge, I accept it on behalf of freedom. We will engage in competition for the virgin soil of Kansas, and God give the victory to the side that is stronger in numbers as it is in right."

The idea of emigrating to Kansas appealed to John Brown Jr., the eldest of Brown's children, who encouraged his brothers Owen, Frederick, Salmon, and Jason to venture westward with him. The elder Brown opted to instead return to North Elba and continue helping his compatriots at Timbucto. Though pleased that his son was "disposed to go to Kansas or Nebraska, with a view to help defeat Satan and his legions," Brown felt "committed to operate in

William H. Seward was one of the most vocal abolitionists in the Senate, and vigorously protested the expansion of slavery into the Kansas Territory. (npg)

Pro-slavery men from Missouri routinely crossed into Kansas to cast illegitimate ballots and intimidate free-state settlers.
(WVSA)

another part of the field," both father and son viewing their decisions to venture east and west as a means of ending the scourge of slavery.

Conditions in Kansas continued to worsen. Pro-slavery men poured into Kansas, intimidating any suspected free-state settlers and upending the first territorial elections in November 1854 and again in March 1855, casting thousands of illegitimate ballots in favor of pro-slavery candidates. Competing pro-slavery and free-state legislatures formed and drafted constitutions, each deeming the other illegitimate. Missouri Senator David Atchison bragged to Jefferson Davis, then Secretary of War, that "we will be compelled to shoot, burn & hang" the free-state settlers. The pro-slavery town of Atchison, Kansas was named in his honor.

In spite of such difficulties, the Brown children and their families arrived in Kansas in two waves in the spring of 1855. They settled at Osawatomie and began improving several tracts of land they dubbed "Brown's Station." Within days of arriving, the Brown clan was harassed by a group of heavily armed pro-slavery men who inquired where the family stood on the issue of slavery. John Jr. replied the family was free state "and more than that, we are abolitionists." Brown recalled, "from that moment we were marked for destruction." Shortly afterwards John Jr. composed a letter to his father at North Elba, imploring the elder Brown to solicit funds from northern abolitionists for the purchase of weapons and ammunition to defend the free-state men from "hundreds and thousands of the meanest and most desperate of men, armed to the teeth with Revolvers, Bowie Knives, Rifles and Cannon." Driving his point home, John Jr. implored that free-state men needed weapons "more than we do bread."

It was late June before John Brown arrived in North Elba and received the letter from John Jr. Brown quickly made preparations to travel west, placing Watson Brown in charge of the North Elba farm and family. With son-in-law Henry Thompson, Brown made several stops on the trip west, including at an abolitionist convention in Syracuse and in Hudson, Ohio, soliciting funds and donations as they traveled. In Hudson, Brown visited his father for the final time, the elder Brown recalling his son exhibited a "warlike" spirit and hoped it would be employed for self defense and "nothing more." Owen Brown expired the following spring as his son fought for life and freedom on the Kansas prairie.

John Brown's father, Owen Brown, imbued his own abolitionist sentiments in his son, but worried about John's "warlike spirit" in Kansas. (wvsa)

The elder Brown reunited with his son Oliver in Chicago, and the three pressed on to Osawatomie, arriving on October 7, 1855. Brown's wagon was laden with supplies, chief among them the arms, ammunition, and swords his son requested many months before. Events in the Kansas territory continued to spiral as cold weather set in. A pro-slavery settler shot and killed a neighboring free-state settler. Rather than arresting the assailant, the local sheriff instead arrested a free-state settler. A free-state mob responded by freeing the prisoner and absconding with the innocent man to Lawrence. Anticipating retribution, Lawrence readied for battle and John

While it had been hoped that the Popular Sovereignty promised by the Kansas Nebraska Act would calm the national climate relating to slavery, it instead stoked wholesale violence across the Kansas plains. (loc)

LIBERTY. THE FAIR MAID OF KANSAS..IN THE HANDS OF THE 'BORDER RUFFIANS'.

SOUTHERN CHIVALRY — ARGUMENT VERSUS CLUB'S.

Violence over slavery was not confined to Kansas. On May 22, 1856, Congressman Preston Brook brutally caned Senator Charles Sumner in the U.S. Senate Chamber. Secret Six Conspirator George L. Stearns paid for Sumner's medical care following the incident. (loc)

Brown led a hastily organized militia to defend the free state bastion. With pro-slavery men poised to attack, cooler heads prevailed and crisis was averted as both sides agreed to deescalate the situation. The so-called "Wakarusa War" ended with no further bloodshed.

In early 1856, free-state settlers snubbed then-governor of the Kansas Territory, Wilson Shannon, who anti-slavery men viewed as "an extreme Southern man in politics, of the border ruffian type," and elected Charles Robinson of Lawrence as governor under the Topeka Constitution, which was drafted the previous year by the free-state legislature to outlaw slavery in the Kansas Territory. John Brown Jr. dipped his toes into politics and was elected to serve as a representative of the legislature. Unfortunately for the free-state faction, Washington viewed Wilson Shannon and the pro-slavery legislature at Lecompton as the legitimate governing body of the territory. It was this body's Lecompton Constitution that aimed for Kansas's admittance as a slave state. With President Franklin Pierce throwing his weight behind the pro-slavery body, it became even more dangerous to be a free-state man traveling to or living within the Territory. As spring rains thawed the Kansas prairie, it seemed inevitable that violence would reignite, and the Brown family soon found themselves marked for certain destruction.

The tinder box exploded on May 21, 1856, when about eight hundred pro-slavery men invaded Lawrence, Kansas, terrorizing citizens and looting property. They vandalized the offices of two free-state newspapers and destroyed the presses. They set fire to the Free State Hotel, the most recognizable symbol of Lawrence's defiance to what its citizens deemed pro-slavery mob law. On their way out of town the mob also burned the home of Charles Robinson, elected governor only several months earlier.

The pro-slavery mob was jubilant. Ringleader Samuel Jones, then Sheriff of Douglas County, gloated that he made the free-state men "bow to him in the dust." Where Jones was exultant, John Brown was enraged. "Now something must be done. We have got to defend our families and our neighbors ... we must show by actual work that ... this thing cannot go on with impunity," Brown demanded before deciding then that "something is going to be done now." He again called up his militia, dubbed the Pottawatomie Rifles. The men were still more than twenty miles away when word reached them that Lawrence had been sacked. The group huddled and discussed these recent developments, undoubtedly believing themselves and their families to be the next targets. Brown felt that the free-soil settlers in Kansas—his own family included—had been terrorized. The time for reprisal was at hand.

On May 24, John Brown gathered four of his sons (Owen, Frederick, Salmon, and Oliver), his son-in-law Henry Thompson, and another local compatriot, Theodore Weiner. While Brown did not divulge his plans, violence was assumed when he directed his sons to sharpen the broadswords he had brought west from Ohio. A local settler was engaged to transport Brown's party to Pottawatomie Creek, near the cabins of several pro-slavery settlers. Under the cover of darkness, the men closed in on their first target, the cabin of James Doyle.

Upon gaining entry to the cabin, Brown and his sons abducted Doyle and his two oldest sons, William and Drury. Against the protestations of Doyle's wife, Brown's gang led the three men into the road a short distance from the cabin, where Salmon and Owen Brown raised their broadswords and slashed at the men, inflicting fatal blows to their heads and torsos. Moving down the road the men next stopped at the home of Allen Wilkinson and announced him their prisoner. After removing him from the cabin, Thompson and Weiner killed Wilkinson with their broadswords before moving on. Crossing Pottawatomie Creek, the men next approached a cluster of buildings and there

Brown's sons, Jason and John Jr., were both captured in the wake of Pottawatomie. (nypl)

apprehended William Sherman, who was summarily executed by Thompson and Weiner.

In short order Brown's "Northern Army" had abducted five men, marched them steps from their beds, and brutally ended their lives within earshot of their loved ones. While they owned no slaves themselves, the five victims were ardent pro-slavery men who had targeted and intimidated their free-soil neighbors. And there's no doubt that Kansas was something of a lawless land, thanks in large part to the fumbling and mismanagement of President Franklin Pierce and his administration in far off Washington, D.C. Yet even the violence and lawlessness that had hallmarked the Kansas territory for years paled in comparison to these murders. Headlines splashed across newspapers north and south, earning John Brown both notoriety and praise. While Brown never confessed to the murders and did not himself wield a broadsword, he spent the remainder of his life with a bounty on his head. To be certain, these murders ushered in the darkest and deadliest days of the Bleeding Kansas conflict.

Following the Pottawatomie massacre Brown and his men took to the woods, anticipating retribution. Brown wrote to his wife and children at North Elba to detail recent events in the territory. John Jr. and Jason had been apprehended; their fate remained uncertain. Pro-slavery men burned Brown's Station. Brown hid from "Missourians & their ruffian allies" who boasted "with awful profanity that they would have our scalps." John Brown's fight for freedom was now also a fight for his life.

On June 1, 1856, Brown's "Northern Army" joined forces with a company of free-state men from

Prairie City (present day Baldwin City) in hopes of protecting that settlement from marauding pro-slavery men roving the countryside in search of Brown. The following morning, the combined free-state forces attacked the pro-slavery men just east of Prairie City at Black Jack. The fighting lasted over three hours, and both sides sustained several casualties, including Brown's son-in-law and Potawatomie accomplice, Henry Thompson.

With mounting losses and pro-slavery men fleeing the battlefield, twenty-four men of the pro-slavery militia surrendered, ending the first protracted battle of Bleeding Kansas. Brown attempted to negotiate a prisoner exchange, wherein free-state men, including his sons John Jr. and Jason, were to be exchanged for his recent prisoners. Instead, three days later, U.S. troops under the command of Col. Edwin V. Sumner arrived at Black Jack to demand that all organized military parties there disband, thus nullifying Brown's plans for a prisoner exchange. Among Sumner's command was a young lieutenant, James Ewell Brown (J. E. B.) Stuart, who three years later would again come face-to-face with Brown at Harpers Ferry.

J. E. B. Stuart later recognized John Brown at the engine house in Harpers Ferry as the same man he had encountered at Black Jack three years earlier. (loc)

Brown and his men went back into hiding "with the serpents of the rocks & wild beasts of the wilderness, being obliged to hide away from our enemies." He nursed Henry and his son Salmon, who was grievously wounded by the accidental discharge of a rifle following the battle, back to health. Despite the failed prisoner exchange, both John Jr. and Jason were released by their captors later that summer. In July, Brown led his "Northern Army" to Topeka, offering protection to the free-state legislature meeting there, and the following month transported his ailing sons out of Kansas to Iowa, hoping to eventually return them to the family settlement at North Elba.

Violence again flared in Kansas in August 1856 as pro-slavery militias poised to attack the free-soil strongholds of Lawrence, Topeka, and Osawatomie. As an army of some 300 Missouri militia approached Osawatomie on August 30, John Brown commanded one of two small companies of free-soil men ready to defend the town. Armed with a cannon charged with grapeshot, the Missourians fired on and charged into Brown's men, concealed in a covered position. Short on ammunition, Brown and his men abandoned the field, hoping the Missourians would chase them rather than destroy the town. Instead of pursuing Brown, the Missourians plundered and torched Osawatomie, leaving smoldering buildings in ruin as they resumed their march towards Topeka.

Even in defeat, Brown escaped with the majority of his command intact. Brown estimated his command inflicted "31 or 32 killed; and from 40 to 50 wounded" on his attackers. Brown's losses were

significantly lighter at five men killed, though Brown felt one loss most painfully. Frederick Brown was shot at the outset of the battle, killed by Reverend Martin White, whom Frederick's older brother Jason believed had the Brown family "marked for destruction" since their arrival in Kansas the previous year, and who had captured and imprisoned both Jason and John Jr. only several months earlier. Indeed, White claimed three years later that "The same day I shot Fred, I would have shot the last devil of the gang . . . if I had known them and got the chance." Frederick Brown was buried on the battlefield at Osawatomie, the first of John Brown's children to die in the war against slavery, though not the last.

In 1877, a monument was dedicated to the men of Brown's command lost at Osawatomie, including Frederick Brown. (nypl)

As John Brown watched Osawatomie burn, Jason recalled his father exclaiming through tears, "God sees it. I have only a short time to live—only one death to die, and I shall die fighting for this cause. There will be no more peace in this land until slavery is done for. I will give them something else to do than extend slave territory. I will carry the war into Africa." Brown now planned to relocate the fight from the Kansas prairie, where slavery was only proposed, to the South, where slavery existed.

Brown's determined stand at Osawatomie in the face of a superior foe earned him further notoriety following the Pottawatomie killings. While southerners viewed Brown as a violent extremist, northern abolitionists saw in Brown a man not confined to words, but who was instead willing to fight. The battle earned him the nickname "Osawatomie Brown." Contradicting this cold-blooded narrative, Brown demurred when presented with the opportunity later that year to kill Reverend White at his home and achieve some measure of retribution for Frederick's death. "I do not harbour the feelings of revenge," Brown said. "I act from a principle. My aim and my object is to restore human rights."

In September 1856, the new territorial governor, John W. Geary, arrived and flexed his muscles with 1,300 Federal troops in an attempt to quell the violence pervading Kansas. After months of near constant movement and conflict, Brown's health began to fail. Wracked with fever and dysentery, Brown slipped out of Kansas the following month, intent on restoring his and his family's health in order to continue the fight.

Kansas had been hard on John Brown and his family. He arrived there only the year before. In leaving, he left the family settlement at Brown's Station and left a son buried at Osawatomie. Yet in that year Brown established both himself and his family as warriors for the cause of freedom, more so than his earlier work at Hudson, Springfield, and North Elba. It was in Kansas that Brown's family was threatened and harassed by Missouri slaveholders and border ruffians. It was Kansas that demonstrated to Brown that politics and compromise would not even halt slavery's expansion, let alone bring it to an end. Kansas also showed Brown the power of the press, which he leveraged to promote his exploits and his cause.

And while Brown would yet return to Kansas, it was 1856 that shifted Brown's attention to the slaveholding south.

"The Slave Will Be Delivered by the Shedding of Blood"

Planning the Raid

CHAPTER TWO
OCTOBER 1856 - JANUARY 1859

While recovering from the emotional and physical toll of the 1856 "Bleeding Kansas" campaign, John Brown was intent on using his newfound notoriety to raise funds to allow him to continue his war against slavery. First, he accumulated arms and accoutrements in Tabor, Iowa, where his son Owen was convalescing. Tabor proved a welcome respite for Brown, the town having been founded by natives of Oberlin, Ohio, where his father had been active years before. At a stopover at the offices of the National Kansas Committee in Chicago, Brown secured 200 Sharps rifles, sending them back to Tabor for storage until spring.

Brown continued on eastward to Hudson and Columbus, Ohio, where he met governor Salmon P. Chase, a future presidential candidate and President Abraham Lincoln's secretary of the treasury. Brown finally arrived in Boston in January 1857. There he presented himself to the Massachusetts State Kansas Aid Society, a relief organization which had raised more than $100,000 to assist free-soil settlers in the Kansas Territory. During his meeting with the society, Brown made the acquaintance of noted abolitionist Franklin Sanborn.

The courthouse in St. Louis where the Dred Scott decision was passed down is now preserved as a national park. (cm)

A Harvard graduate, Sanborn was only 25 years old but had thrown himself entirely into the Kansas cause. A sojourn to the Kansas Territory in 1856 convinced Sanborn that Kansas represented "the most practical form in which the struggle for freedom has ever presented itself." Already familiar with Brown's Kansas exploits, Sanborn introduced Brown to other prominent abolitionists of Boston, including wealthy industrialist and philanthropist George Luther Stearns, Unitarian ministers Theodore Parker and Thomas Wentworth Higginson, and noted physician Samuel Gridley Howe. In the following years these men, with Brown's earlier associate, the wealthy philanthropist Gerrit Smith, would play a prominent role in the planning and execution of the attack on Harpers Ferry. In fact, of their many combined accomplishments, it is instead their relationship with John Brown that continues to define these men—dubbed The Secret Six—to this very day. Sanborn remained the most determined defender of Brown's memory and legacy, penning the definitive *Life and Letters of John Brown, Liberator of Kansas, and Martyr of Virginia* in 1885.

Brown also met for the first (and only) time with William Lloyd Garrison, editor of the anti-slavery newspaper *The Liberator*, of which Brown was a reader. Both men worked for the immediate emancipation of slaves but their shared vision likely ended there. Where Garrison argued for nonviolent measures, John Brown did not believe that words alone would move the dial on slavery. "Talk is a national institution," he said, "but it does not help the slaves." Brown was a man of action. "I have been at your abolition meetings," Brown told one abolitionist, "and your scheme is perfectly futile. You would not release five slaves in a century; peaceful emancipation is impossible; the thing has gone beyond that point." While Garrison later criticized the attack on Harpers Ferry, his tone softened following Brown's execution, arguing "John Brown executed will do more for our good cause . . . than John Brown pardoned."

Brown continued to New York City for a meeting of the National Kansas Convention before going on a speaking tour across the northeast, raising funds to purchase necessary arms and equipment. He also visited his family toiling at North Elba, his first visit there since June 1855. The family struggled during his absence, subsisting on what little money Brown sent home and what could be obtained from friends.

Though operating at different ends of the abolition spectrum, in an era otherwise dominated by compromise, both William Lloyd Garrison and John Brown sought an immediate end to slavery in the United States. (loc)

Brown leaned on his new abolitionist acquaintances in Boston to further see to his family's needs in his absence, which came sooner than they hoped.

By May, Brown was on his way back to the Kansas territory, woefully short of the arms and funds he had hoped to raise. Yet all was not lost. In March, Brown made the acquaintance of Hugh Forbes, an English mercenary with ties to Italian revolutionary Giuseppe Garibaldi. Promising payment of $100 per month, Brown secured Forbes's services to produce a military manual and travel with him to the territory to train his men for renewed combat. Brown also contracted with a Connecticut blacksmith to fabricate one thousand six-foot pikes with double-edged blades at a cost of $1.00 per pike. While only a handful of these pikes were used in the raid at Harpers Ferry, they have become one of its most recognizable symbols.

At the expense of her health and finances, Mary Ann Brown endured long periods without her husband. Annie Brown, at left, later joined her father at the Kennedy farmhouse and spent the rest of her life defending her father's legacy. (loc)

Upon arriving back in Tabor later that summer, Brown found that the situation in Kansas had cooled considerably during his absence. Governor Geary resigned and was replaced by attorney Robert J. Walker of Mississippi, one-time Secretary of Treasury in the Polk administration. An October election passed peaceably, with announced Free State candidates earning a majority of seats in the territorial legislature.

When Forbes arrived at Tabor that August, he was surprised to find that John Brown and his son Owen were the only troops on-hand to drill. As Brown began to unpack his plan for 'lightning raids' along the Alleghenies—first proposed to Frederick Douglass a decade earlier—the personalities between the two strong-willed men began to clash. Where Brown proposed that freed slaves would join his forces, Forbes argued to send them on to Canada and freedom. Forbes departed Tabor after one month and would become a certain thorn in Brown's side in the coming months.

Following Forbes's departure, Brown ventured into Kansas, meeting with anti-slavery militants who, like him, had settled in the territory to swing Kansas towards the free-soil cause. No doubt using his notoriety gained at Pottawatomie and Osawatomie,

While most popular images of Brown show his flowing white beard, Brown was clean shaven during most of his Kansas campaign. (npg)

Brown recruited nine men, several of whom would play key roles in the yet-to-be-revealed attack on Harpers Ferry, including John H. Kagi, John E. Cook, Aaron D. Stevens, Charles P. Tidd, and William H. Leeman. These men immigrated to Kansas from Maine, Connecticut, Massachusetts, and Ohio, and all were active in anti-slavery activity in the territory. Leeman was a familiar face, having fought with Brown at Osawatomie, while both Stevens and Kagi had served in a company of free-soil militia. Kagi had been seriously wounded in a fight with a pro-slavery judge and was "long in recovering from his wounds." Brown wanted men who "feared God too much to fear anything human," and he believed he had found them.

Conveying his army back to Tabor, Brown made startling revelations to the men. He showed them the cache of weapons he had stockpiled, including rifles, revolvers, and ammunition. He also shared that the work for which the men had been recruited would not be found in neighboring Kansas, but rather in distant Virginia, where they would strike at the very heart of slavery. Finally, he revealed that he must soon depart Tabor and return east to do more fundraising for the Virginia expedition. Without Hugh Forbes to train his army, Brown left Aaron Stevens in charge, quartering the men for the winter near the Quaker community of Springdale, Iowa. Stevens, a former US dragoon and Mexican War veteran was more recently captain of the Second Kansas Free State Militia and was Brown's best hope to mould his recruits into fighting shape.

Shipping the arsenal to Ohio for safekeeping, Brown himself headed east, arriving in Rochester, New York in late January 1858. He stayed there for three weeks as a guest of Frederick Douglass, using the time to draft a "Provisional Constitution and Ordinances for the People of the United States." The document became the framework for the structure and laws of the free state Brown aimed to create somewhere in the mountains of the South. In the preamble to the Constitution, Brown declared slavery as "barbarous, unprovoked, and unjustifiable." He invoked the language of the country's founding documents as well as the previous year's *Dred Scott v. Sandford* case, in which the Supreme Court ruled that Congress had no authority over slavery in the territories and that slaves are not citizens of the United States. Brown instead argued, "We, citizens of the United States and the Oppressed people . . . declared to have no rights which the White Man is bound to respect; together with all other people degraded . . . establish ourselves . . . to protect our Persons, Property, Lives and Liberties." Among the forty-eight articles outlining the new government, Brown focused on the institution of slavery, decreeing that the property of slaveholders would be "confiscated and taken, whenever and wherever it may be found."

Brown also undertook a letter writing campaign, urging his family to keep the faith while soliciting

In a 7-2 decision, the Supreme Court ruled that Dred Scott, and all African Americans for that matter, had "no rights which the white man was bound to respect." (loc)

LEFT: Franklin Benjamin Sanborn introduced Brown to four other members of the Secret Six and remained an unapologetic defender of Brown and his actions until his death in 1917. (wvsa)

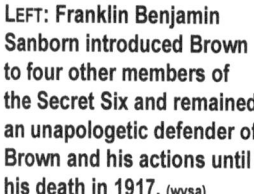

CENTER: A wealthy industrialist and philanthropist, Secret Six conspirator George Luther Stearns provided significant financial backing for Brown's operations. He later served as a recruiting agent for several Black regiments during the Civil War, including the famed 54th Massachusetts. (wvsa)

RIGHT: A wealthy philanthropist who helped to found the African American settlement at North Elba, Gerrit Smith also served to bankroll Brown's activities and suffered a mental breakdown following Brown's raid. (npg)

donations from his wealthy friends. In February, he traveled to the Peterboro, New York, estate of Gerrit Smith for a meeting with Smith and Sanborn. While careful not to mention Harpers Ferry as his target, Brown outlined his plans for a strike against slavery in the Old Dominion, inciting a "grand rescue" that would topple slavery in its largest stronghold. Invoking scripture, Brown exhorted the men that "if God be for us, who can be against us?" His plans satisfied Smith, who would tell Sanborn "we must support him. . . . I see no other way." Smith excitedly wrote to Ohio abolitionist Joshua Giddings that "the slave will be delivered by the shedding of blood—and the signs are multiplying that his deliverance is at hand."

In March, Brown traveled to Boston, where over the course of four days he detailed his plans to Higginson, Howe, Parker, and Stearns, just as he had earlier related to Smith and Sanborn. The news elated Higginson, who was "always ready to invest money in treason," while Stearns had vowed to "devote my life and fortune to this cause." Cautiously optimistic of Brown's success, the six men formed a secret committee and offered Brown the financial backing of $1,000. Sanborn admitted, "Without accepting Brown's plans as reasonable, we were prepared to second them merely because they were his." This pledge of financial support, and even their association with Brown, cost these men dearly in the years to come. However for Brown, not only was he loosening purse strings, he was changing minds as to how slavery should be eradicated.

Brown continued a tour of the northeast with stops at Philadelphia, Brooklyn, Syracuse, and back home at North Elba, only his second visit there over the past year. During his nine day stay, Brown related his Virginia plans to yet another audience and secured

commitments from his sons Oliver and Watson, as well as Dauphin and William Thompson, brothers of his son-in-law and Kansas compatriot Henry Thompson. Brown's army slowly grew.

Crossing the border into Canada, Brown first visited St. Catherines, Ontario, the northern terminus of one important Underground Railroad line and the home of famed conductor Harriet Tubman. He was most impressed with Tubman after his meeting with her, writing to his son John Jr. that she was "the most of a man, naturally, I have ever met with." Brown continued on to Chatham, Ontario, the symbolic northern terminus of the Underground Railroad and home to more than 1,000 African Americans, both fugitive and free. Chatham was a beacon of opportunity for free and escaped African Americans. It offered schools, worship and social institutions. Here, Brown visited Dr. Martin Delany, a Harvard-educated physician and a noted abolitionist and Underground Railroad conductor. Brown knew that Delany could organize Chatham's African American community and asked for his help.

Telling Delany he would return in May, Brown quietly returned to Iowa in April 1858 to gather his troops, now reinforced by two new recruits added during his absence. Rather than eastward, he instead shepherded his men north into Canada. Brown knew that his small army could not deliver slavery themselves, nor should it be an army of only white men. Brown needed to enlist both escaped slaves and freedmen in his cause, not only for their numbers but to show that this was a united strike against the institution of slavery.

Aaron Stevens had kept the men busy during Brown's absence, instructing them in target practice, swordsmanship, and military maneuvers, as well as

LEFT: **An avowed Transcendentalist and abolitionist, Secret Six conspirator Theodore Parker defended Brown's actions and likened Brown to a martyr and saint. Parker died in Italy in 1860.** (wvsa)

CENTER: **Secret Six conspirator Thomas Wentworth Higginson was not only an activist in the cause of abolitionism, but an advocate for women's rights, workers rights, and temperance. During the Civil War, Higginson served as Colonel of the 1st South Carolina Infantry, the first regiment of free Black men authorized for Federal service.** (wvsa)

RIGHT: **Boston physician Samuel Gridley Howe was another Secret Six conspirator. Howe was an active member of the Boston Vigilance Committee, helping to protect escaped slaves from slave catchers. Howe helped to fund Brown's activities, and fled to Canada following the raid to escape persecution.** (wvsa)

First meeting in 1858, Brown revered Harriet Tubman as the bravest person on the continent, though she ultimately decided against participating in Brown's raid on Harpers Ferry. (npg)

studying *The Patriotic Volunteer*, the manual compiled by Hugh Forbes. Their minds were kept fresh with rhetoric, mock debates, and a literary library. Ingratiating themselves into the Quaker community, the men even welcomed two new recruits: Barclay and Edwin Coppoc, Ohio natives who traveled west as teenagers. While Barclay had spent time in Kansas, he missed the vicious fighting over slavery, espousing the nonviolence tenet of his Quaker faith. However, by 1858, the brothers were prepared to deliver slavery by the sword.

It was at back Chatham, Canada, on May 8 that Brown convened his Constitutional Convention, disguised as a Masonic meeting. The convention, Brown hoped, would ratify the Provisional Constitution he had promulgated only several months earlier. Brown was likely disappointed to find no familiar faces from his New England invitees, including Frederick Douglass, in whose home Brown drafted the constitution. However, Martin Delany held his end of the bargain, delivering 34 African American delegates to the convention. These men—there were no women in attendance—paired with Brown's 11 white men met for three days to debate the merits of the document.

Martin Delany chaired the meeting, while John H. Kagi served as secretary. Brown again delivered his plans to attack slavery. While the delegation overwhelmingly supported Brown's plans for an armed assault, they did push him on several issues. How would Brown's army evade capture in the mountains? Could slaves be counted on to rise up and make war on their former masters? Martin Delany challenged Brown on these and other issues, causing Brown to offer a stinging rebuke, saying "Gentlemen, if Dr. Delany is afraid, don't let him make you all cowards."

After spirited debate, the provisional constitution was ratified on the third evening of the convention. The governing document of John Brown's theorized nation was approved. On the final day of the convention, the delegates elected officers, naming Brown as Commander-in-Chief and Kagi as secretary of war. Brown enlistees Richard Realf and George B. Gill were elected secretaries of state and treasury, while Owen Brown was elected Treasurer. Two members of Congress were elected: Alfred Ellsworth and Osborne Anderson.

While many Chatham attendees later fought for the Union Army, most notably Martin Delany, Brown counted only one Chatham recruit who was present at Harpers Ferry—Osborne Perry Anderson. A Pennsylvania native, Anderson was a printer by trade and abolitionist by avocation. In Chatham he was employed by Mary Ann Shadd Cary, a prominent abolitionist and publisher of the *Provincial Freeman* newspaper. Anderson believed that Brown was intent on "destroying the tree that bringeth forth corrupt fruit. Slavery was to him the corrupt tree, and the duty of every Christian man was to strike down slavery, and commit its fragments to the flame."

While Brown was planning his new government, Hugh Forbes resurfaced. First, he demanded recompense from members of the Secret Six and the Massachusetts Kansas Committee, including Franklin Sanborn and Samuel Gridley Howe. He wrote to Horace Greeley of the *New York Tribune* and made his way to Washington, D.C., cornering prominent Republicans including New York Senator William H. Seward and Massachusetts Senator Henry Wilson. Wilson was incredulous to the information Forbes offered up—a conspiracy to incite servile insurrection in Virginia, possibly through the misappropriation of state funds. He demanded answers from the

Following his interactions with Brown, Delany recruited for the United States Colored Troops during the Civil War and became the first commissioned African American officer in the Union Army. (npg)

committee leadership, throwing the Secret Six into a panic. Gerrit Smith was despondent, writing "Brown must go no further. . . . [I]t would be madness to attempt to execute it," Thomas W. Higginson was defiant, stating "when the thing is well started, who cares what he [Forbes] says?"

The group recalled Brown to Boston, where over two days in late May he met at the Revere House with Sanborn, Howe, Parker, Stearns, and Smith. Higginson, an avowed disunionist, was the only member absent, believing "any postponement as simply abandoning the project." At the meeting, the Secret Six reached several decisions to which Brown reluctantly agreed. Brown's proposed strike into Virginia, planned to step off after the Chatham Convention, was suspended for at least a year. Brown was to return to Kansas and make his presence there known, which would discredit Forbes's betraying allegations. Brown was not to share the details of any plans with the group, thereby protecting them from indictment. He would keep the two hundred Sharps rifles provided to him two years earlier by the Massachusetts Kansas Committee, then stored in an Ohio warehouse. Upon his eventual return east in 1859, Gerrit Smith vowed to provide him with $2,000, no questions asked. A dejected Brown stated to Higginson, the only Secret Six member opposed to delaying the attack, that his fellow committee members were "not men of action."

Brown first stopped at North Elba to visit his wife and children before traveling to Ohio, where he met with his men who had been patiently waiting there since departing Chatham the previous month. Instructed to remain steadfast and ready, the men scattered from Ohio to await further orders from Brown. John H. Kagi, Brown's newly-minted secretary of war, and Charles Tidd traveled with Brown back to Kansas, while others returned to Iowa. Richard Realf, Brown's secretary of state, was to track down Hugh Forbes to ensure he did not publicly reveal Brown's plans. John E. Cook relocated to Harpers Ferry, where he would obtain maps, ingratiate himself into the community, and report back to Brown on the number and disposition of slaves in the area. This was the first hint about where Brown planned for his blow to fall and what would be involved in the attack.

By the end of June, Brown, Kagi, and Tidd arrived back in Kansas, where Brown found simmering tensions reignited. The previous December, the pro-slavery

Hugh Forbes's betrayal of Brown's plans to Senator Henry Wilson (above) and other politicians led the Secret Six to delay Brown's Virginia campaign. (loc)

legislature adopted the Lecompton Constitution, which aimed to open the Kansas Territory to slavery. Thousands of pro-slavery men crossed from Missouri to tip the scales in their favor. But Congress refused to ratify the constitution, instead ordering a new and more orderly election for August 1858.

On May 19, 1858, a group of 30 pro-slavery men crossed the Missouri border into Linn County, Kansas, killing five free soil men and wounding five others. Dubbed the Marais des Cygnes ("Marsh of the Swans") Massacre, the nation was horrified at the renewed bloodshed. Poet John Greenleaf Whittier penned a heartfelt poem about the massacre for the *Atlantic Monthly*. "Henceforth to the sunset, unchecked on her way; shall liberty follow, the march of the day," Whittier waxed, referencing the victims as "unarmed and unoffending."

Brown was incensed and within days relocated to Linn County, writing to Franklin Sanborn that "it seems the troubles are not over yet." Raising a company of fifteen men, Brown, using the alias Shubel Morgan, occupied a farm overlooking the Missouri border. There, he began construction of a stone and log fort—dubbed Fort Snyder—designed to protect free soil settlers from similar incursions. "Confidence seems to be greatly restored amongst the Free State men," Brown wrote to his son, warning that "Missouri people along the Line might have perfect quiet if they honestly desired it . . . and if they chose War they would soon have all they might . . . care for." Territorial governor James W. Denver worked to secure a truce, hoping to avert further bloodshed before the August 1858 territorial election.

A sometime poet and lecturer, Richard Realf joined with John Brown in Kansas and was later named secretary of state in Brown's Provisional Government. Realf was not present at Harpers Ferry and committed suicide in 1878. (wvsa)

On August 2, Kansas settlers voted overwhelmingly against the Lecompton Constitution by nearly a 10,000-vote margin, effectively assuring that Kansas would be admitted to the Union as a free state. Brown continued to patrol the Missouri border, adding two men to his Harpers Ferry force. Indiana native Jeremiah Anderson moved to Kansas the previous year and was active in the free state cause. Albert Hazlett was born in Pennsylvania and was an ardent abolitionist, writing "I am willing to die in the cause of liberty, if I had ten thousand lives I would willingly lay them all down for the same cause." Brown called on several of his men to reconvene in Kansas should any further violence flare up.

After hearing the appeal of a Missouri slave, Brown took his war into the slaveholding south for the first time. On December 19–20, 1858, Brown crossed into Missouri with two companies of men, one under his command and the other under his drillmaster Aaron D. Stevens. Brown's company first descended on the home of Harvey B. Hicklan and freed a family of Hicklan's slaves. The men then moved to the neighboring farm of John Larue, freeing an additional five slaves. In the process, the raiders also took Hicklan and Larue hostage.

Stevens's company proceeded to the nearby farm of slave-owner David Cruise. After gaining entry to the home, Stevens shot and killed Cruise after the man leveled a pistol. One slave was freed as a result. The companies conducted the liberated slaves into Kansas and returned to the border to prepare for certain retaliation. Stevens wrote, "we are right. . . . [W]e will resist if the whole universe is against us." An elated Brown stated, "Observe, I have carried the war into Africa." An exasperated Missouri governor Robert Stewart offered a $3,000 bounty for Brown's capture, to which President James Buchanan offered an additional $250, despite the fact that Brown had not committed nor directed the murder. Brown later mocked Buchanan, offering a mere $2.50 for the president's capture.

As tensions calmed over the winter of 1859, Brown shepherded the freed slaves north to freedom. Tracked by a pro-slavery company of some 45 men, Brown, Kagi, Stevens, and George Gill were joined by a handful of free soil men from Topeka. On January 31, 1859, near Holton, Kansas, the pro-slavery men caught up with Brown's group at the swollen Straight Creek, intent on capturing Brown and collecting the substantial bounty. Arming the slaves, Brown instead drove his band straight across the creek and into the waiting posse, scattering the group and capturing several horses and four prisoners, all without firing a shot. Free state settlers in Kansas satirized the affair as "The Battle of the Spurs," mocking the pro-slavery men who fled the scene on horseback.

Brown proceeded to Tabor, Iowa, where disgruntled residents drafted a resolution admonishing Brown. It stated that they had "no sympathy with those who…take property or life." Continuing on, Brown secured a railroad boxcar to carry the group to Chicago, where, with the assistance of noted detective Allan Pinkerton, they traveled on to Detroit. There, on March 12, eighty-two days and more than one thousand miles since their liberation by Brown's forces, the former slaves boarded a ferry to Canada. The press was full of news of Brown's exploits. An elated Gerrit Smith wrote his wife, "Our dear John Brown is invading Kansas [Missouri] and pursuing the policy which he intended to pursue elsewhere." Sanborn wrote to fellow Secret Six member Thomas W. Higginson that "he has begun the work in earnest . . . we may look for great results from this spark of fire." Brown had demonstrated that he was capable of such a "lightning strike" into a slaveholding state as he first proposed to Frederick Douglass a decade earlier. His strike into Virginia, as proposed to his financiers nearly a year before, now seemed feasible.

Before leaving Detroit, Brown met with Frederick Douglass, William Webb, George DeBaptist, and other prominent African Americans. The group met Brown's Virginia plan with tempered enthusiasm. Douglass opposed the plan and promised only financial support. This was a blow to Brown. Others in the group proposed more drastic measures, including a plot to blow up substantial churches in the south on a given Sunday. Brown demurred—his plan in Virginia called only for self defense should he be attacked.

Now Brown headed east to collect the funds promised from Gerrit Smith and the Secret Six the previous year. His campaign in Kansas ended, he felt assured that Kansas would "have no more attacks from Missouri." His exploits at Pottawatomie, Osawatomie, Black Jack, and the raid into Missouri garnered him both notoriety and praise. Dr. Charles W. Robinson, head of the New England Emigrant Aid Company, one-time free-soil governor, and future governor of the state of Kansas, wrote Brown to comfort him that "History will give your name a proud place on her pages" for his "prompt, efficient, and timely action against the invaders . . . and murderers." In taking his leave of Bleeding Kansas, Brown himself offered a chillingly accurate farewell: "I shall now leave Kansas; probably you will never see me again; I consider it my duty to draw the scene of the excitement to some other part of the country."

"We Will Proceed to the Ferry"

To the Kennedy Farmhouse

CHAPTER THREE

JANUARY 1859 - OCTOBER 16, 1859,
EVENING

It was not by accident or coincidence that John Brown dispatched John Edwin Cook to Harpers Ferry in the spring of 1858. The small town situated at the confluence of the Potomac and Shenandoah rivers was actually a well selected and attractive target from which Brown could initiate his war on slavery. Founded in 1763, the site had attracted visitors for decades, both for use of the ferry crossing on the Potomac River and for the picturesque beauty of the area, dominated on three sides by majestic bluffs. Thomas Jefferson visited the area in 1783, remarking that the site was "one of the most stupendous in nature" and that the scene was "worth a voyage across the Atlantic."

The American Revolution demonstrated to President George Washington the need for national armories that could produce arms and ordnance for the fledgling nation. In 1794, Congress approved legislation that provided for the establishment of up to four armories, though only two were created. Washington believed that Harpers Ferry, with its proximity to the District of Columbia, reliable water power, vast forests, and mineral deposits made it "the most eligible spot on the whole river in every point of view." By 1796, the government had purchased 125 acres of land at Harpers Ferry for construction of the second national armory, the first having been

The Kennedy farmhouse was designated a National Historic Landmark in 1974 and underwent extensive restoration to return the building to its 1859 appearance. (jeg)

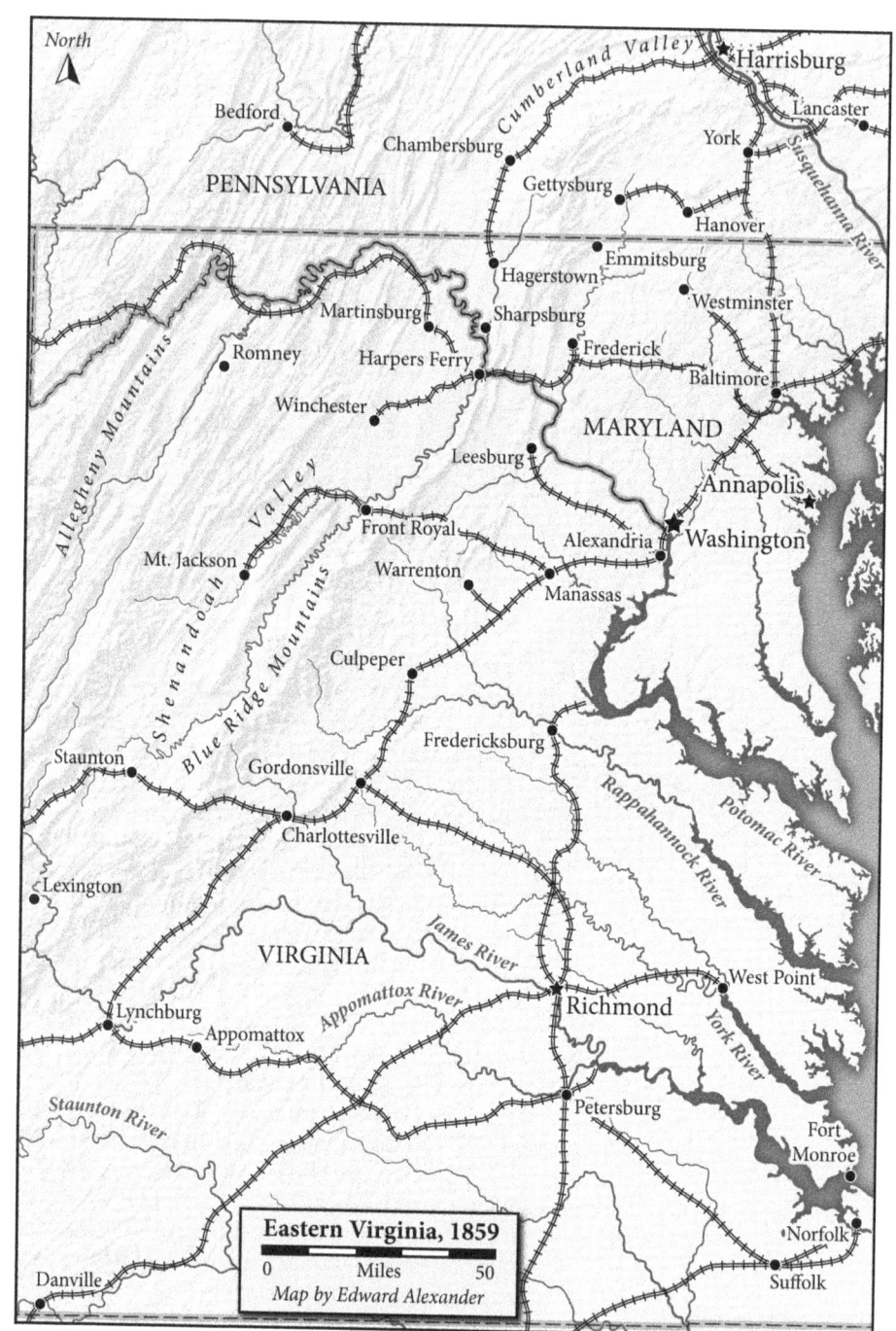

EASTERN VIRGINIA, 1859—First visiting the Harpers Ferry area nearly twenty years prior to the raid, John Brown envisioned the local mountain ranges as a conduit to transport slaves north to freedom. Brown believed "a thousand men in the mountains" could not defeat his smaller command, a strategy he also employed in Bleeding Kansas.

established at Springfield, Massachusetts two decades earlier. Within its first decade the armory at Harpers Ferry had produced thousands of firearms, including muskets and pistols.

As production increased so did the footprint of the armory, extending from the banks of the Potomac River to the banks of the Shenandoah. Gunsmith John Hall constructed Hall's Rifle Works on an island in the Shenandoah River near the town. Instituting uniformity in his production process, Hall was a pioneer in interchangeable parts, revolutionizing the weapon-making business at Harpers Ferry and helping to usher in the Industrial Revolution. The War Department later acquired Hall's property and there built a modern rifle factory. The mid-1840s witnessed an overhaul of the entire armory complex; dilapidated, fire-prone wood buildings were replaced with uniform brick structures. The armory employed more than 400 workers, many of them immigrants from Ireland and Germany, swelling the town's population to 3,000 souls by 1850.

Harpers Ferry was also a transportation hub. The Shenandoah Canal sluiced through the village, while the Chesapeake & Ohio Canal skirted the opposite bank of the Potomac River. The C&O Canal was quickly followed by the Baltimore & Ohio and Winchester & Potomac railroads. The namesake ferry across the Potomac was usurped by a modern railroad bridge in 1837, connecting Harpers Ferry to points west. Turnpikes facilitated improved road travel to neighboring towns and villages as transportation and water power attracted more industry to Harpers Ferry, including an iron foundry and several mills.

While located only 40 miles from free soil in Pennsylvania, Harpers Ferry remained firmly within slavery's grasp. The 1860 census, enumerated the year after John Brown's Raid at Harpers Ferry, counted nearly 4,000 slaves in Jefferson County, more than a quarter of the entire population of the county. Neighboring Virginia counties—Clarke, at nearly 3,400 slaves (47% of county population), and Loudoun, at nearly 5,500 slaves (25% of county population), as well as counties to the north in Maryland, likewise

At the time of John Brown's Raid, the Harpers Ferry armory employed some 400 workers. On April 18, 1861, the armory was destroyed to keep the equipment from falling into the hands of Virginia troops. (loc)

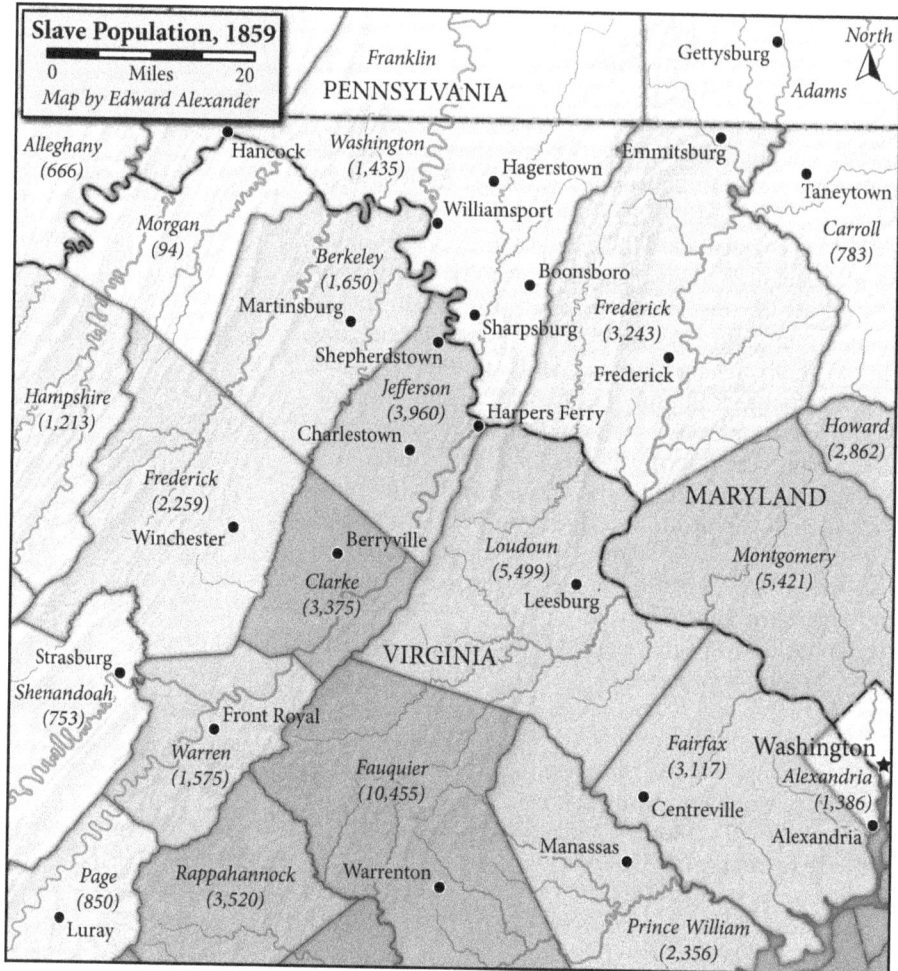

Slave Population, 1859
0   Miles   20
Map by Edward Alexander

PENNSYLVANIA
Franklin
Gettysburg
North
Adams

Alleghany
(666)
Hancock
Washington
(1,435)
Hagerstown
Emmitsburg
Taneytown

Morgan
(94)
Williamsport
Carroll
(783)

Berkeley
(1,650)
Boonsboro

Martinsburg
Sharpsburg
Frederick
(3,243)

Shepherdstown
Frederick

Hampshire
(1,213)
Jefferson
(3,960)
Harpers Ferry

Charlestown
Howard
(2,862)

Frederick
(2,259)
MARYLAND

Winchester
Berryville
Loudoun
(5,499)
Montgomery
(5,421)

Clarke
(3,375)
Leesburg

Strasburg
VIRGINIA

Shenandoah
(753)
Front Royal
Fairfax
(3,117)
Washington

Warren
(1,575)
Fauquier
(10,455)
Alexandria
(1,386)

Centreville
Alexandria

Manassas

Page
(850)
Rappahannock
(3,520)
Warrenton
Prince William
(2,356)

Luray

SLAVE POPULATION, 1859—Another reason why Brown chose Harpers Ferry as his target was the high density of counties with sizable slave populations surrounding the town. In Jefferson County, Virginia, and the counties immediately adjacent, lived some 21,421 slaves.

boasted enticing numbers of slaves whom John Brown could pluck from captivity.

By 1859, African Americans accounted for approximately 10% of the town's population, split evenly with approximately 150 enslaved and 150 free. The free population in town included the likes of Heyward Shepherd, a Winchester resident who served as baggage handler for the Baltimore & Ohio Railroad at Harpers Ferry, while others worked as blacksmiths and laborers. Brown hoped this local free population could assist his army in liberating those still enslaved.

Even so, not all Harpers Ferry residents believed that African Americans should be, or even desired to be, free. Reverend Peter Costello, pastor of St. Peter's Catholic Church, perched above the lower town, believed "slaves are much better off than the free Negroes, and they know this to be the fact, hence it is that they prefer to remain as they are, and it is better for them, I am sure."

From John Brown's time living in Springfield, Massachusetts, he understood that the armory at Harpers Ferry contained the arms and ammunition needed to equip the slaves he was sure would rally to him. The arsenal at Harpers Ferry in fact housed some 100,000 firearms, a prize greater than Brown could likely have envisioned. Paired with significant local slave populations and situated close to the Mason-Dixon line, Harpers Ferry proved an enticing target from which Brown could shuttle slaves north to freedom. The mountainous topography of the South Mountain range and the Allegheny Mountains further to the west offered Brown the ideal terrain to launch his "lightning raids." Believing he could destabilize the slave market in the border south, Brown hoped economics would prove more lethal to slavery than the sword.

Even still, the risks were high in attacking a government installation. President Buchanan, whose reward money for Brown's capture, based on his earlier activities in Kansas, remained unclaimed, would certainly bring all the resources at his command to bear on Brown. An attack on government property would certainly prove more an affront to Buchanan than Brown's mocking reward money. Troops stationed in Washington, D.C., while limited in number, could be entrained and dispatched to Harpers Ferry within hours. Having evaded Federal cavalry in Kansas, Brown would need to again rely on both speed and cunning to evade capture at Harpers Ferry.

But Brown knew the local climate. His Secretary of War, John Kagi, once taught school in the neighborhood, while confidant Martin Delany had been born in neighboring Charlestown (present day Charles Town, West Virginia). Armed with this inside information and having decided on his target, Brown dispatched John Edwin Cook to Harpers Ferry, where he arrived in June 1858. Cook secured a room in a boarding house in the neighboring community of Bolivar and went to work as a school teacher and a tutor. He also worked as a lockkeeper on the canal, allowing him to keep an eye on the nearby armory. In less than a year, he married a local girl, Mary Virginia Kennedy, who bore him a son in the spring of 1859.

While Cook ingratiated himself into the Harpers Ferry community, Brown continued to solicit both funding and support for his planned

With a bounty on his head following his Kansas campaign, Brown grew out his now-recognizable beard to conceal his true identity as he returned east. (npg)

Virginia campaign. After leaving Detroit, he spent several weeks in Ohio, brandishing a bowie knife and auctioning horses captured at the Battle of the Spurs. Traveling on to New York, he met with Gerrit Smith at Peterboro. Elated at Brown's recent successes in Kansas and Missouri, Smith provided $400 towards Brown's plans. At Boston, George Luther Stearns, having earlier sworn his fortune to assist Brown, provided an additional $1,200. While the money was certainly appreciated, Brown needed more men to fill his ranks. "It is men I want, and not money," lamented Brown. "Money I can get plentiful enough, but no men. Money can come without being seen, but men are afraid of identification with me, though they favor my measures."

From Boston, Brown traveled to Collinsville, Connecticut, to call on blacksmith Charles Blair. Brown had contracted with Blair two years earlier to produce 1,000 pikes with which he planned to arm the slaves he would liberate. Not having received payment, Blair halted production at 500 and stored the pikes, hopeful to eventually recoup his losses. Brown arrived with the necessary funds to produce a total of 954 pikes. He instructed Blair to forward the pikes to Chambersburg, Pennsylvania, Brown's planned supply base.

By June 1859, Brown returned to North Elba, his first visit in a year, and ultimately his last. His family remembered him visibly changed from the last time they saw him. The Kansas Campaign had taken a physical toll on Brown. Fever, chills, and ague wracked his body, leaving him prostrate for weeks at a time. A defiant Brown, however, remarked, "I would rather have the small pox, yellow fever, and cholera all together in my camp, than a man without principles."

Most noticeably, Brown had grown a flowing white beard, concealing his features from would-be captors. While his family trimmed the beard before his departure from North Elba, it remains today his most distinctive and recognizable feature, captured in a photo in a Boston studio the month before. Meeting Brown in Boston, Bronson Alcott, father of Louisa May Alcott, believed the beard gave Brown "a soldierly air and the port of an apostle," recalling that in spite of sickness Brown appeared "agile and alert. . . . I think him about the manliest man I have ever seen."

At North Elba, Brown supplemented his meager army with his son Oliver and William Thompson, younger brother of Brown's son-in-law and Kansas compatriot Henry Thompson. Watson Brown pledged to rejoin his father's command following the birth of his first child that summer. Brown and Oliver traveled from North Elba to Akron, Ohio to pick up Owen Brown. There, John Jr. had been secreting the cache of Sharps rifles and Maynard revolvers, waiting for his father to call for them. That time had come, as Brown made arrangements with John Jr. to transfer the Sharps rifles and revolvers to Chambersburg.

As the seat of Franklin County in south-central Pennsylvania, just north of the Mason-Dixon line, Chambersburg had a long history as a stop on the Underground Railroad. The county had one of the highest concentrations of free African Americans anywhere in

John Brown and Frederick Douglass met in a quarry near this site in Chambersburg in August 1859. Douglass declined to join Brown, but Shields Green opted to "go wid de ole man." (jeg)

FREDERICK DOUGLASS
AND JOHN BROWN

The two abolitionists met at a stone quarry here, Aug. 19-21, 1859, and discussed Brown's plans to raid the federal arsenal at Harpers Ferry. He urged Douglass to join an armed demonstration against slavery. Douglass refused, warning the raid would fail; the Oct. 16, 1859 attack confirmed his fears. Brown was captured with his surviving followers and was executed Dec. 2, 1859.

Pennsylvania Historical Marker marking the quarry site, located along Conococheague Creek on West Loudoun Street (Route 30). (jeg)

the state, the neighboring community of Mercersburg even having a district known as "Little Africa." Brown's Chatham confidant Martin Delany had spent his youth in Chambersburg and likely provided Brown with information on the local population. Thus, Chambersburg was on Brown's radar as a staging point for his Virginia campaign. John Jr. had been his agent in the area, his father directing him in early 1858 to find "every person and family of the reliable kind" in "Bedford, Chambersburg, Gettysburg, Hagerstown, Md. or even Harpers Ferry, Va.," noting "when you look at the location of those places, you will readily perceive the advantage of getting up some acquaintance in those parts."

Brown, Oliver, and Owen arrived in Chambersburg in June 1859, assuming the name Isaac Smith & Sons. They secured lodging at the Ritner Boarding House, owned by Mary Ritner, widow of a son of the former governor of Pennsylvania, Joseph Ritner. Brown's lodging was located just a few blocks from the village diamond and within view of the Cumberland Valley Railroad, on which his shipments and recruits arrived. From there Brown could also see the warehouses where he stowed his armaments of war.

Perhaps Brown knew that Mary Ritner and her late husband had themselves been active on the Underground Railroad. Her daughter, Emma Jane Ritner, later recalled John Brown as "strong and vigorous. I think it was only his white hair and beard that caused us to think of him as an older man." Emma and her sister would often ride with John Brown for a mile or two south of town before walking back, not realizing he was transporting weapons and ammunition.

At the Ritner Boarding House, Jeremiah Anderson, a loyal compatriot from Brown's Kansas campaign, joined Brown and his party. In Chambersburg, Brown received his stockpile of weapons from John Jr., shipped in crates as "hardware & castings" and "household goods." The pikes from Connecticut did not arrive until the fall. John Henry Kagi also reached Chambersburg, where he remained until shortly before the raid. Kagi assumed the name "John Henri," though he bragged that he could have given locals a name they "will always remember." Emma Ritner recalled that John Kagi "wrote beautifully and mother had him give us instruction in penmanship."

The party arrived in Harpers Ferry for the first time on July 3, 1859. There, Brown briefly conferred with John E. Cook, the first time he had seen Cook in more than a year. Entrusting Cook to remain vigilant and discreet, the party retired across the Potomac River to Sandy Hook to spend the next night. The following day, Independence Day, the men traveled across Maryland Heights, the imposing precipice dominating the lower town of Harpers Ferry.

On the road from Harpers Ferry they happened upon a local farmer, John Unseld, and inquired about property prices in the neighborhood. Identifying himself as Isaac Smith, a farmer and cattle purveyor from New York, Brown remarked that the area was "a very fine country, a very pleasant place," and that he might prefer to rent property before buying. Unseld suggested a vacant farmhouse approximately five miles from Harpers Ferry, owned by the heirs of Dr. Booth Kennedy.

Brown liked the property. The log and stucco home included a living room and two bedrooms,

The Ritner Boarding House served as a gathering point for John Brown and his men from June–October 1859. The house is today operated as a museum by the Franklin County Historical Society. (jeg)

Martha joined her husband Oliver Brown at the Kennedy farmhouse in the summer of 1859. Pregnant by the time she departed the farmhouse, both Martha and the child expired in the winter of 1860. (wvsa)

an expansive attic, and a cellar, as well as a separate smaller cabin elsewhere on the property. Perhaps most attractive was that the house sat back from the road, which would protect the inhabitants from prying eyes. Brown negotiated a lease through March of 1860, securing the house and cabin, use of the pasture, and firewood, at the cost of $35 in gold. Brown's forward base of operations now shifted from Chambersburg to the Kennedy farmhouse.

In anticipation of the arrival of his army, Brown needed women—preferably his wife Mary, and daughter, Anne—to join him. Having first explained that his wife had been left in New York until the sale of their property concluded, he now required her presence in Maryland to help quell any suspicions to the comings and goings of various men from the property. Sending Oliver to New York to escort them, Brown wrote to Mary, pleading, "I find it will be indispensible [sic] to have some women of our own family with us." Perhaps realizing she would demur, he was willing to accept Anne and Oliver's wife, Martha Brewer, though he implored Mary that "it will be likely to prove the most valuable service you can ever render to the world." Though wishing "health and success in the great and good cause you are engaged in," Mary declined her husband's call, but reluctantly allowed Anne, then only 16 years old, and Martha, 17, to accompany Oliver back to Maryland.

The trio arrived at the Kennedy farmhouse by mid-July, sharing one of the two bedrooms in the humble cabin. The two girls tended to the household duties, including baking, washing dishes, sewing, and gardening. It was Anne's (more commonly known as Annie) duty to keep Brown's army concealed, and she kept a close eye on any wandering passersby, recalling later how her father had called her his "watch dog," reminding her that she "must not let any work interfere with my constant watchfulness." A neighboring family, the Huffmasters, proved to be a "pestering torment" for Annie. They lived within view of the exterior stairwell and tended a rented garden just behind the Kennedy farmhouse. Annie described her time at the Kennedy farmhouse as akin to "standing on a powder magazine, after a slow match had been lighted."

Watson Brown and William and Dauphin Thompson arrived on August 6. True to his word, Watson had departed North Elba following the birth of his first child, a son named Frederick in honor of his brother, who had been killed at Osawatomie, Kansas three years earlier. Watson had been spared the violence of Kansas, staying home to help his mother at the North Elba homestead. Harpers Ferry would be his first and only campaign. The Thompson brothers, siblings of Brown's son-in-law and Kansas compatriot, Henry Thompson, were two of eighteen children born to the Thompson family and were eager to join Brown's small army. Their brother Henry, still recovering from his Kansas wound, opted to stay home with his wife.

Annie later recorded her experiences at the Kennedy farmhouse during the summer and fall of 1859. Offering a rare glimpse into the day-to-day life inside the cramped quarters, she captured thoughtful, if not frank, observations of the various men who made up her father's army as they arrived at the farmhouse, dubbing them "my invisibles." Of the Thompson brothers, Annie remembered William as "easy-going, good-natured . . . kind hearted and generous to a fault," while of Dauphin, who fancied Annie, she recalled, "was a quiet person, read a good deal, said little. . . . innocent as a baby." The brothers, along with Watson Brown and Jeremiah Anderson, lodged in the small cabin on the property, opposite the farmhouse.

By mid-August, Brown's army began to take shape at the farmhouse. Brothers Edwin and Barclay Coppoc arrived. Annie remembered Edwin as "caring for and fearing nothing...no better comrade have I ever met." She found Kansas veteran Charles Plummer Tidd uneducated and "by no means handsome." The quick-tempered Tidd often found himself at odds with Annie's father. This disaffection soon boiled over into near mutiny.

Aaron Stevens, Brown's Kansas drillmaster, also arrived at the farmhouse in August, as did Kansas veterans William Leeman, whom Annie remembered as "only a boy . . . very handsome and very attractive," and Albert Hazlett, whom Annie believed "knew he was going to his end" in joining Brown's army. Leeman and Hazlett proved difficult to contain at the farmhouse, often wandering about during daylight hours, sometimes straying as far as Harpers Ferry.

Stewart Taylor, a young Canadian who in 1853 had emigrated to Iowa, where in 1858 he met John Brown, also arrived in August. Described as "heart and soul in the anti-slavery cause," Taylor removed to Illinois after participating in the Chatham Convention. There, John Kagi recalled him to Brown's army. An exuberant Taylor wrote, "It is my chief desire to add fuel to the flame."

Finally, in late August or early September, Brown received a new recruit from eastern Ohio: Dangerfield Newby, a 39-year-old African American. Of all Brown's enlistees, Newby is the most evocative, his portrait perhaps the most recognizable of all the Harpers Ferry raiders next to John Brown himself. Born in Fauquier County, Virginia to a white father and an enslaved mother from a neighboring plantation, Dangerfield, his mother, and his siblings remained slaves until late 1858 when his father relocated the family to Belmont County, Ohio. An 1856 Ohio Supreme Court case (*Anderson v. Poindexter*) had set a precedent, that for those formerly enslaved who establish residency in Ohio, slavery's "manacles instantly break asunder and crumble to dust."

In emigrating to Ohio, Dangerfield was forced to leave behind his wife, Harriet, and their six children,

John Brown's oldest son, John Brown Jr., served with his father in Kansas, but was not present at Harpers Ferry, instead serving as his father's liaison and recruiting agent. During the Civil War, he served in the Seventh Kansas Cavalry and died in 1895. (wvsa)

who remained in bondage at a Brentsville, Virginia, plantation. Dangerfield entered negotiations with their owner, hoping to secure Harriet's freedom at up to $1,000.00. Harriet's owner, not believing her husband could raise that amount, goaded Newby in a letter that he should instead return to slavery if he hoped to reunite his family. In Ohio, Newby connected with a local politician and visited local meetings and congregations, begging for money to free his family, ultimately raising more than $700.00. When negotiations broke down, Newby decided to reclaim his family by force. While liberating the enslaved was a moral calling for John Brown and his men, for Dangerfield Newby, it was much more personal.

Agonizing letters from Harriet to Dangerfield were recovered following the raid. Harriet implored him to rescue her and reunite their family. In April 1859, Harriet begged, "oh Dear Dangerfield, com [sic] this fall without fail, monny [sic] or no monney [sic]." Two weeks later, she told her husband to "com [sic] as soon as you can for nothing would give me more pleasure than to see you." By August, Harriet's pleadings were more dire, pleading Dangerfield to "buy me as soon as possable [sic] for if you do not get me somebody else will. Dear Husband you [know] not the trouble I see. It is said Master is in want of monney [sic]. If so I know not what time he may sell me an then all my bright hops [sic] of the futer [sic] are blasted for there has been one bright hope to cheer me in all my troubles, that is to be with you, for if I thought I shoul [sic] never see you this earth would have no charms for me."

Their mission aside, the occupants at the Kennedy farmhouse still found time for simple pleasures. Annie enjoyed "watching the fireflies in the evening and looking at the lights and shadows on those fine old trees and the mountain ridge upon moonlight nights." The men passed the daylight hours reading, debating, playing checkers and cards, and singing. Stevens continued instructing the men in tactics and drilled them to the extent their cramped quarters would allow. Nighttime storms were looked forward to, as the men could "jump about and play, making all kinds of noise . . . as they thought no one could hear them."

In mid-August, Brown's much looked for weapons began arriving in Chambersburg, where John Kagi forwarded them on to the Kennedy farmhouse. The crates were stored around the house and in the cabin on the property where some of the men lodged. The freight due on these shipments threatened to bankrupt Brown's campaign, forcing him to again call on the Secret Six to supplement his funding. His financial backers contributed only $50 but pledged more in the future.

August proved a difficult month at the Kennedy farmhouse. Brown, ever secretive in planning, had concentrated his enlistees in the Maryland countryside without definitive details on where he would lead them. Now Brown began to unpack his plans to the group— slipping into Harpers Ferry and holding the town and government facilities while slaves and hostages were gathered. From there they would strike plantations, gathering slaves and retreating back to the mountains, the sort of lightning strikes that had long appealed to Brown. Annie recalled that her father believed "the slaves would come to them, or the slaveholders would surrender them to gain peace."

On the plan of attacking a government installation, his army was divided. Some, including Kagi and Stevens, on whose input Brown placed great value, favored the plan. Cook also favored the plan, having spent more than a year in the area scouting and examining the armory complex, noting their "contents, weak or strong points, habits of their watchmen, and other matters of value."

In what must have pained their father, Owen, Oliver, and Watson all opposed the plan, as did Annie. Owen likened the plan to Napoleon's march on Moscow, telling his father "I believe that in your anxiety to see that all is going well . . . you will so expose yourself as to lose your life." The loudest objections came from Charles Tidd, who believed they would be surrounded at Harpers Ferry. He later acknowledged that these disagreements "nearly broke up the camp." Tidd packed his belongings, left the farmhouse, and lodged with John E. Cook for a week in Bolivar before returning.

A dejected Brown was willing to both temporarily abandon the campaign and tender his resignation as commander-in-chief of the army he created. He allowed discussions to take place without him and vowed to accept whatever decision the others reached. Owen demurred, believing "we have gone too far... we must go ahead." The men returned their decision within five minutes by way of a note to Brown, which read, "We have all agreed to sustain your decisions, until you have proved incompetent, and many of us will adhere to your decisions, so long as you will."

Owen later recalled that while the men "were not satisfied with the reasons he gave for making our first attack there, all controversy and opposition to the plan from that time was ended."

*   *   *

With one crisis averted, Brown continued to work feverishly during the late summer and early fall to supplement his meager army. Brown dispatched John Jr., who was unwilling to commit himself to further warfare, to instead gather recruits in northeastern Ohio, Detroit, and in Canada, where at Chatham he secured Osborne Anderson, who had pledged his support during the convention there in 1858. John Jr. also visited Boston, where he met with several members of the Secret Six. George Stearns spoke for the increasingly impatient group looking for action on the Virginia front, asking John Jr. to tell his father "that we have the fullest confidence in his endeavor, whatever may be the result."

For John Brown's most prized recruit he could leave nothing to chance. Brown had long courted support from his old friend, activist, and anti-slavery crusader Frederick Douglass. He now called on him to join his Virginia campaign. Brown called Douglass to Chambersburg, where from August 19—21 they met in an old stone quarry southwest of town. There, Douglass found John Kagi and Brown, the latter disguised as a fisherman.

Douglass recalled the meeting years later—Brown unpacked his plans for Harpers Ferry and explained the weapons he would use to arm the slaves who would surely rally to him. "Come with me, Douglass," Brown urged, promising to defend Douglass with his own life. "When I strike, the bees will begin to swarm, and I shall want you to help hive them." Yet Douglass demurred, believing that such an attack on a federal institution "would array the whole country against us." As Brown touted the advantages of seizing Harpers Ferry, Douglass could see only "a perfect steel trap, and that once in, he would never get out alive; that he would be surrounded at once and escape would be impossible." Douglass again refused to join in Brown's quest.

While Douglass recalled these events with the benefit of hindsight—his autobiography was not released until 1882—he was never quite sure whether it was "my discretion or my cowardice" that stayed his participation in Brown's army. Douglass also gave a well-attended lecture on "the Slave Question" while in Chambersburg, attended by both Brown and Kagi.

Even still, Brown did not depart Chambersburg empty-handed. When Brown lodged with Frederick Douglass in early 1858, he met Shields Green, an escaped slave from South Carolina. Douglass recalled Green, sometimes known as "Emperor," as having courage and self-respect that "made him quite a dignified character." Brown asked Douglass to bring Shields Green to Chambersburg. There, after hearing Brown's plans and Douglass's demurral, Green replied when Douglass asked him what he would do "I b'leve I'll go wid de ole man," signaling his enlistment in Brown's army. Green later related to Owen Brown "Oh, what a poor fool I am! I had got away out of slavery, and here I have got back into the eagle's claw again!"

While his army grew at the farmhouse, Brown's spy at Harpers Ferry continued his undercover work. John E. Cook worked to identify the location of local plantations and numbers of both free and enslaved African Americans. He befriended local slaveowner Lewis Washington, the great-grandnephew of George Washington, who possessed several prized Washington relics. Cook, posing as a Kansas buffalo hunter, admired the weapons and secretly planned to one day seize them as spoils of war. Cook also monitored the nearby home of Washington's friend and fellow slave-owner, John Allstadt.

Osborne Anderson arrived at Chambersburg on September 20 and reached the Kennedy farmhouse five days later. Annie Brown recalled that Anderson was "accustomed to being confined in the house, being a printer by trade, so that he was not so restive as some of the others." The men occupied their time assembling the recently-arrived pikes and bronzing their rifles, while Dangerfield Newby worked on a nearby farm. Annie recalled that Newby would "get very low spirited and impatient at what appeared to him the long delay and preparation." Newby undoubtedly chafed at waiting, especially after receiving Harriet's heartrending letters. Now he was so close to his enslaved wife and children in nearby Prince William County. Newby coaxed his brothers in Ohio to join him in Maryland, though he did not disclose any of the group's plans.

As the September days shortened and the men became fully apprised of their destination, the farmhouse took on a more solemn tone. Summer had seen the men writing confident, if not boastful, letters to friends and family, passed through their faithful postmaster at Chambersburg, John Kagi. Young William Leeman was perhaps the most brash, writing to his mother that he was in a "Secret Association... with the sole purpose of the extermination of slavery," and promised, "I am now in a Southern slave state and before I leave it, it will be a free state." Fearful that loose lips might upend his plans, Brown chastised the men and penned Kagi, "I do hope all corresponding except on business of the Co. will be dropped for the present . . . any person is a stupid fool who expects his friends to keep for him that which he cannot keep himself."

Unknown to Brown, an Iowa Quaker had attempted to alert Secretary of War John B. Floyd to Brown's intentions. The Iowan told Floyd that "a secret association," had formed, "having for its object the liberation of the slaves at the South by a general insurrection." David Gue, writing anonymously, tabbed Brown as the leader. Remarkably, Gue had many of the facts correct—that Brown had been recruiting in Canada; that he planned to arm the liberated slaves; even that Brown would "pass down through Pennsylvania and Maryland, and enter Virginia at Harpers Ferry." However, Gue made one critical error in identifying the possible target as an armory in Maryland rather than Virginia. Knowing that no armory existed in Maryland, Floyd presumably dismissed the letter as a hoax.

All of this—talkative men, snooping neighbors, dwindling funds, a lack of new recruits—weighed on Brown. Realizing he could not wait for the men and the funds to arrive, he began to make final preparations for the invasion. In late September, he sent Annie and Martha back to North Elba. On their last night at the farmhouse, the men serenaded the girls, with whom they had become close during their time together. Martha was now expecting a child and was undoubtedly aggrieved to leave her husband, Oliver. The girls departed the farmhouse on September 29, accompanied to Chambersburg by Watson and as far as Troy, New York by Oliver, who then returned to his post. While switching trains in Harrisburg, Annie saw her father returning from a brief trip to Philadelphia with John Kagi. "It was the last time I ever saw father," Annie recalled. She would not look upon his body after he was returned to North

After unknowingly dismissing a warning of Brown's plot, secretary of war Floyd shipped arms to southern arsenals and later served as a general in the Confederate army. (loc)

Elba, instead preferring to "remember him just as we parted" at the train station.

If summer correspondence from the farmhouse was crowing, September and October found the men steeling their resolve, if not resigning to their fate. Aaron Stevens wrote to a friend in Ohio "not knowing that it may be the last time . . . for we commence work in a few days." Watson Brown wrote to his wife, "we are all eager for the work, and confident of success," before admitting, "I sometimes think perhaps we shall not meet again." A defiant Dauphin Thompson chided his family in North Elba. "I suppose the folks think we are a set of fools but they will find out that we know what we are about," he said. John Brown likewise wrote to his family at North Elba, encouraging them to carefully read the newspapers while also acknowledging that they "may not always be certainly true, however." He also spoke directly to his daughter, Annie, who had served him so faithfully at the Kennedy farmhouse. He encouraged her "to become a sincere, humble, earnest, and consistent Christian," and asked her to keep the letter as a remembrance of him.

Three final reinforcements joined Brown's army in October. First was Francis Jackson Meriam, grandson of famed Boston abolitionist Francis Jackson, former president of the American Anti-Slavery Society. Only twenty-two years old, Meriam was described as "enthusiastic, and resolute" and "as absolutely fearless as he was personally unrestrained in his hostility to slavery." Yet Meriam was also of feeble health, suffering from emotional swings and partial blindness. His ability to withstand a prolonged campaign was questionable, yet he contacted Brown in late 1858 offering himself "in any capacity you wish to place me as far as my small capacities go," promising to pay all of his own expenses and "acquire the use of the proper tools for the work" Brown had planned.

The Secret Six sent Meriam to the Kennedy farmhouse, themselves uncertain of his abilities. Thomas Wentworth Higgison later described Meriam as "half-crazy," while Samuel Gridley Howe observed Meriam "in a state of mental excitement bordering on insanity." Meriam brought with him a purse of $600 in gold, funds sorely needed by Brown. He met with Brown and Kagi in Philadelphia before traveling to Baltimore. Perhaps understanding the danger he faced, Meriam had an attorney in Chambersburg draft a will. Meriam's attorney recalled, "after making a few special bequests, [Meriam] gave his property to the

Abolition Society of his native State." Meriam finally arrived at the Kennedy farmhouse on October 15 and brought much needed supplies, including percussion caps and primers for Brown's army and the remaining $250 in gold to sustain their operations.

Lewis Sheridan Leary and John Anthony Copeland also arrived at the Kennedy farmhouse, the last of the much hoped for "express packages" (African American volunteers) to arrive from Chambersburg. John Jr. recruited both men at Oberlin, Ohio, in the summer of 1859, though lack of funds kept them from joining Brown's army until the fall.

Lewis Sheridan Leary was born in North Carolina and moved to Oberlin in 1857, where he worked as a saddle and harness maker. The following year he participated in the highly publicized Oberlin Rescue, in which an anti-slavery crowd forcibly liberated a runaway slave who was being detained under the Fugtive Slave Act before he could be returned to slavery. Copeland, Leary's nephew, was born free in North Carolina in 1834 and relocated to Oberlin as a child, where he attended Oberlin College and became involved in anti-slavery activities. Copeland played a prominent role in the Oberlin Rescue and shepherded the freed slave, John Price, on to Canada, much as John Brown had done with the slaves he liberated on his Missouri raid.

In the final days before the raid, Brown recalled his two outside agents to the Kennedy farmhouse. Brown first sent a note to John Cook, instructing him to "get every thing ready to come with your wife to my home," warning Cook to "be very careful not to say or do anything which will awaken any suspicion" and not to "let any of our plans leak out." Cook's wife and child traveled to the Ritner boarding house at Chambersburg. Young Mary Virginia Cook believed she would only be there a few days before reuniting with her husband for a trip to Kansas. Long-term boarder John Kagi settled her at the boarding house before leaving for the Kennedy farm himself. "The moon is just right" to begin the campaign, Kagi wrote to John Jr.

With the arrival of recruits Meriam, Leary, and Copeland, Brown now had 21 men under his command as he prepared to set his plan into motion. Several days earlier, he drafted "General Orders No. I" from "Headquarters, War Department, Provisional Army, Harpers Ferry," wherein he laid out the organization of his army. On October 15, Brown,

This Civil War view of Harpers Ferry shows the town from the Maryland side of the Potomac River. The stone abutments were all that remained of the bridge used by Brown and his men to enter Harpers Ferry.
(wvsa)

as Commander-in-Chief, conferred commissions to his officers, including Kagi as Secretary of War and Watson Brown as a Captain.

The following morning, Sunday, October 16, Brown prayed with his men, and after breakfast called the roll before convening a council of war, with Osborne Anderson serving as chair. The Provisional Constitution, drafted at the Chatham Convention one year earlier, was read; some of Brown's men heard it here for the first time. Additional commissions were extended, including Cook, Stevens, Tidd, and Oliver Brown as Captains and Leeman, Hazlett, Anderson, Edwin Coppoc, and William and Dauphin Thompson as lieutenants. Anderson recalled, "every man there assembled seemed to respond from the depths of his soul, and throughout the entire day, a deep solemnity pervaded the place."

That afternoon, Brown distributed his marching orders. He ordered Owen Brown, Francis Meriam, and Barclay Coppoc to remain at the farmhouse, with instructions to bring forward arms and equipment when called for. The rest of the men were to proceed quietly in column, being careful to conceal their arms. Tidd and Cook would disable the telegraph lines into Harpers Ferry, while Kagi and Stevens were to secure the bridge watchman, with Watson Brown and Stewart Taylor holding the Potomac Bridge and Oliver Brown and William Thompson holding the Shenandoah Bridge.

Jeremiah Anderson and Dauphin Thompson received instructions to convey prisoners to the armory's engine house while Albert Hazlett and Edwin Coppoc secured the United States Armory. Brown tasked John Kagi and John Copeland with securing the rifle factory on Hall's Island. Aaron Stevens would lead John Cook, Charles Tidd, Osborne Anderson, Shields Green, and Lewis Leary into the country to secure hostages, chiefly Colonel Lewis Washington.

As the day waned, Brown imparted his final instructions to his men. "And now, gentlemen, let me impress this one thing upon your minds. You all know how dear life is to you, and how dear your life is to your friends. And in remembering that, consider that the lives of others are as dear to them as yours are to you. Do not, therefore, take the life of any one, if you can possibly avoid it; but if it is necessary to take life in order to save your own, then make sure work of it."

The conditions on that Sunday night likely fit the "solemnity" described by Anderson. A light drizzle fell, chilling the air, while clouds obscured the moon and stars. At 8:00 pm, Brown pulled on his cap and called out, "Men, get on your arms; we will proceed to the ferry."

A Nation's Armory

You are standing directly across the street from the main entrance of one of the nation's first military-industrial complexes. The U.S. Armory at Harpers Ferry, now covered by an embankment of dirt and rubble, produced the deadliest weapons of its day. From the early 1800s until the start of the Civil War, in 1861...Gutted during the Civil War, the armory was later razed and mostly covered with rubble to make way for elevated train tracks. A stone obelisk on the rise in front of you marks the original location of what became known as John Brown's Fort.

John Brown's Fort (above right) in its original location on the armory grounds during the Civil War.

"They Say They Have Come to Free the Slaves"

The Raid Begins

CHAPTER FOUR

OCTOBER 16, 1859, EVENING -
OCTOBER 17, 1859, MORNING

The men marched in pairs, spaced apart at intervals. No one uttered a word. Besides the fall of their boots on the road, the column made no sound; the men marched "as solemnly as a funeral procession." Each raider concealed his weapons—Sharps carbines, revolvers, and knives—beneath his clothing.

For two hours, the silent procession marched through the rolling western Maryland countryside that, finally, dropped toward the Potomac River. The column turned left and followed the road along the river. Off to their right, as they moved farther downstream, the faint gas lights of Harpers Ferry came into view. A waning full moon revealed the industrial town at the junction of the Potomac and Shenandoah rivers. There rested the reason for this secret nighttime march: weapons—approximately 100,000 of them—that these raiders came to confiscate. Those firearms were the tools they hoped to use to redeem four million slaves in the American South.

As the column neared the bridge carrying the Baltimore & Ohio Railroad across the Potomac River into Harpers Ferry, the raiders' breaths shortened. Each man gripped his weapon tighter, knowing the task was soon at hand.

The site of the armory gate is covered by the late 19th century railroad embankment erected in lower town Harpers Ferry. (kp)

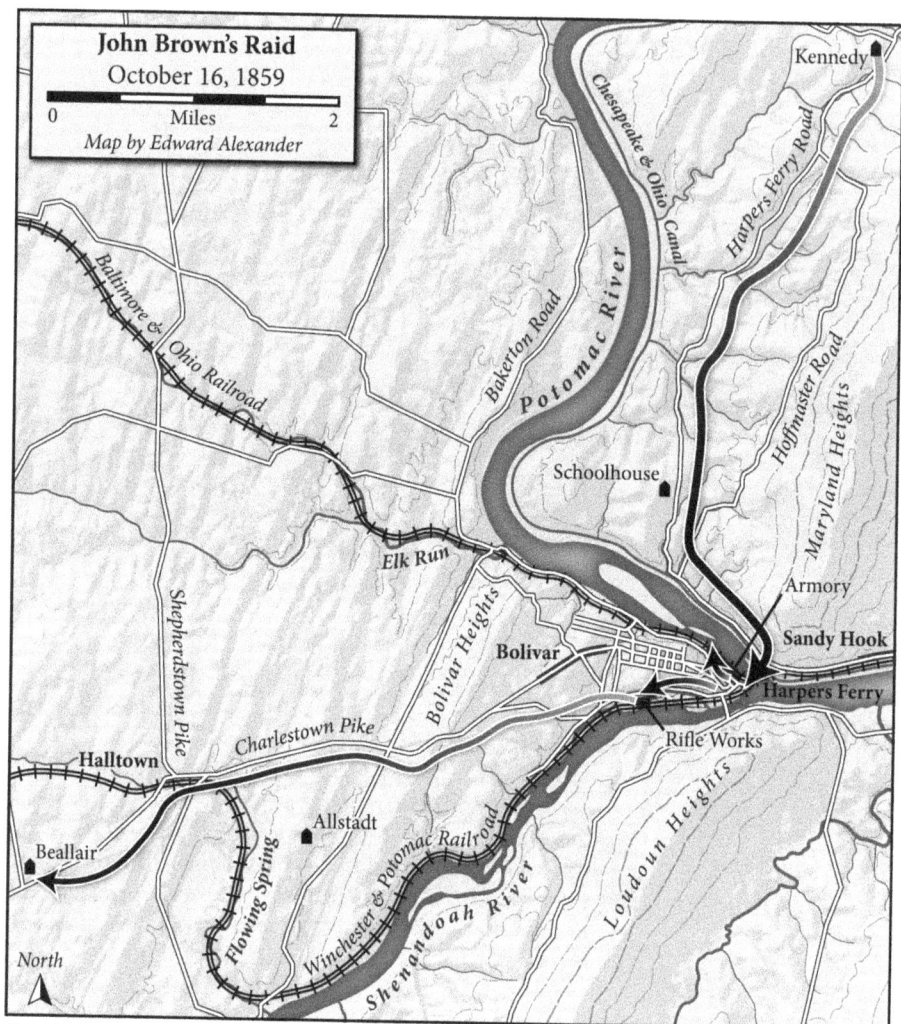

John Brown's Raid
October 16, 1859

0   Miles   2

Map by Edward Alexander

JOHN BROWN'S RAID—Brown's raiders used the cover of night to travel undetected to Harpers Ferry from the Kennedy farm. (ea)

Arriving at the bridge, Brown, seated in the wagon near the column's head, ordered his command to halt. The men knew the signal as they unslung their accouterments and secured them "outside of our clothes." Brown's second in command, John Kagi, and one of his captains, Aaron Stevens, readied their carbines and moved onto the bridge.

Once the two men entered the bridge from the Maryland side, lone watchman Bill Williams, lantern in hand, approached the two silhouetted strangers. Kagi and Stevens waited until Williams was close enough before they captured him. With little trouble, the raiders had secured their route into Harpers Ferry.

Led by Brown in his wagon, the raiders proceeded across the Potomac and into Virginia. The wagon wheels rumbling across the bridge and onto the street in front of the armory gate alerted armory watchman Daniel Whelan that a party was approaching. Whelan glanced at his watch—10:45 p.m.

The faint light in the armory yard showed Whelan that a wagon was parked in front of the gate. Believing the visitor was the head watchman, Whelan left his post in the fire engine house and strolled to the iron gateway. The chain that locked the gate rattled, signaling Whelan that the party wished to gain entrance into the armory yard. "Hold on," the watchman yelled.

When he reached the gate, he did not recognize any of the individuals standing before him. "Open the gate," they demanded. Whelan refused. Suddenly, one man jumped onto the stone pillar the gate was anchored to while another thrust his hand through the gate itself and grabbed Whelan. Quickly, more men approached and shoved the muzzles of their guns into Whelan's breast. From a position of clear strength, the strangers once more commanded that the gate be opened. Whelan refused one last time.

"We have no time to be waiting for a key," piped up a voice from the wagon. "Grab the tools," the commanding voice ordered. A crowbar was produced and with a few twists of the chain, the shackle snapped. The way into the arsenal was open; the wagon and men on foot forced their way into the armory yard. The men shoved their guns into Whelan's face, ordering him to remain silent.

Whelan heard the same commanding voice barking out orders to the raiders. After dispersing his force throughout the town and surrounding countryside, the leader, whom Whelan later identified as Brown, said, "I came here from Kansas, and this is a slave State; I want to free all the negroes in this State; I have possession now of the United States armory, and if the citizens interfere with me, I must only burn the town and have blood."

Brown's men quietly took possession of the eastern portion of the armory yard by 11:00 p.m. Shortly thereafter, the command secured the nearby arsenal and the rifle factory on Hall's Island along the Shenandoah River. Pickets patrolled the bridges across both rivers. Brown's plans had thus far succeeded smoothly.

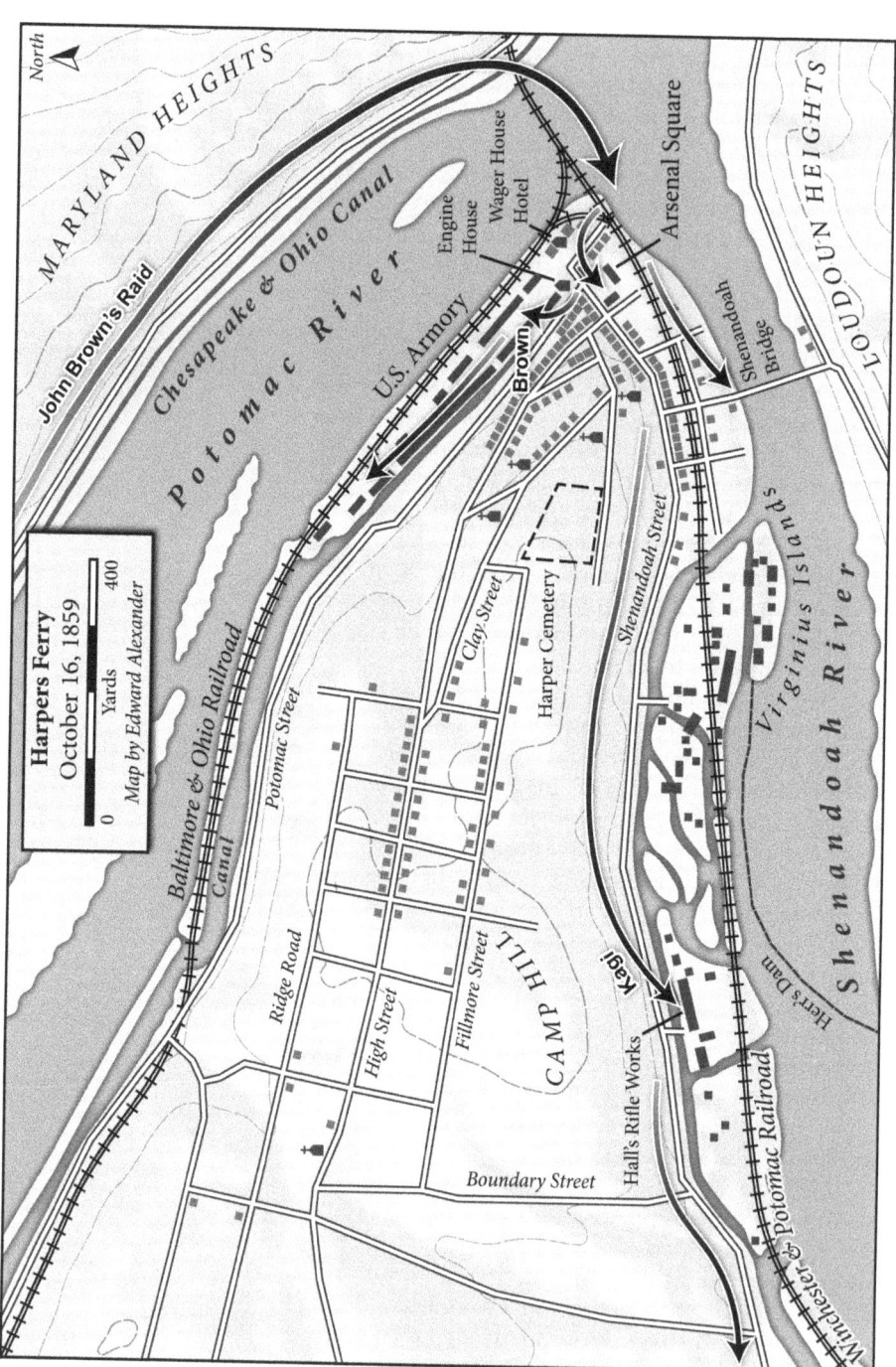

North

MARYLAND HEIGHTS

John Brown's Raid

Chesapeake & Ohio Canal

Potomac River

Engine House

Wager House Hotel

Arsenal Square

Brown

U.S. Armory

Shenandoah Bridge

LOUDOUN HEIGHTS

Harpers Ferry
October 16, 1859

Map by Edward Alexander

0   Yards   400

Baltimore & Ohio Railroad

Canal

Potomac Street

Clay Street

Harper Cemetery

Shenandoah Street

Virginius Islands

Shenandoah River

Ridge Road

High Street

Fillmore Street

CAMP HILL

Kagi

Hall's Rifle Works

Herr's Dam

Boundary Street

Winchester & Potomac Railroad

Aside from those scattered throughout the government factories in the lower town, Brown dispatched five raiders under Capt. Aaron Stevens to the surrounding countryside to rouse the local slave population and capture prisoners. Included in this group was Brown's eyes and ears in Harpers Ferry, John Cook. He knew the surrounding countryside and was also familiar with the primary target on Brown's list: Colonel Lewis Washington, the first president's great-grandnephew.

Four weeks earlier, Cook had traveled to Washington's 670-acre plantation—Beall-Air— between Charlestown, and Harpers Ferry. During his visit, Cook curried favor with the honorary colonel, even engaging him in a friendly shooting contest. The spy also inspected two of Washington's highly prized possessions that were likewise coveted by Brown: a pistol presented to George Washington by the Marquis de Lafayette and a sword gifted to the general by Frederick the Great. The belongings of America's revolutionary founding father resonated with Brown's own desire to begin a revolution, and the colonel's slaves would, in Brown's plan, constitute the first men to rise up and join Brown's command.

On their way to Beall-Air, Stevens's command— two white men and three black men—met a handful of black men. The raiders told them of their purpose, which the men supported. Stevens dispersed them to spread the word about Brown's arrival in Virginia to secure their freedom.

By 1:30 a.m., October 17, the six raiders arrived at Beall-Air. Their loud knocks on the plantation home's rear door received no reply. The visitors forced the door open with a fence rail and entered the hallway, shouting Washington's name. Awakened by these voices, Washington opened his bedroom door, clothed only in his "night-shirt and slippers," and was immediately greeted by three carbine muzzles and a revolver. Four armed men illuminated by a single torch stood in Washington's doorway.

"Is your name Washington?" asked one of the party. "That is my name," replied the colonel. When Cook confirmed the prisoner's identity, Stevens told him, "You are our prisoner." Stevens then told the colonel to dress. While he did so, the raiders ransacked Washington's gun chest and grabbed the Washington family relics Brown had asked for. They also tried to pilfer some of the colonel's personal possessions, including his watch, to which he replied, "You have set yourselves up as great moralists and liberators of slaves; now it appears that you are robbers as well."

As Washington dressed and prepared for the cold five-mile ride to Harpers Ferry, members of the raiding party liberated Washington's slaves and "borrowed" Washington's two-horse carriage and a four-horse wagon to make their return to Harpers Ferry with their captured prizes..

Not far from Beall-Air, Stevens's returning party stopped at the recently widowed Mrs. Henderson's house. Washington implored them not to wake the family at this time of night, as the lone occupants were Mrs. Henderson and her daughters. Apparently satisfied, the wagons continued east without stopping.

They next halted about 3:00 a.m. in front of the home of John H. Allstadt, which was adjacent to the Charlestown Turnpike. Like his neighbor, Colonel Washington, Allstadt was a prosperous farmer; the 1860 census counted seven slaves and nearly $50,000 worth of property. Stevens's men resorted to a familiar tool—a fence rail—to gain entry to the Allstadt's home.

Once the raiders jarred the door loose, Lewis Washington heard "a shout of murder and general commotion in the house" from his perch in his carriage. Allstadt's daughters screamed in a fit of panic at the sudden intrusion. The alarm shook Allstadt from his slumber. A sharp reply shot back that this band of men had captured the armory at Harpers Ferry and were going to take Allstadt, his son, and his slaves there. Most importantly, they told him of their grand plans: "Free the country of slavery."

The father and son quickly dressed and left the comfort of their warm beds for a seat in a wagon on a cold October morning. Stevens and his men had already gathered Allstadt's slaves by the time the men emerged from the house. "The negroes were all armed with pikes," the elder Allstadt remembered, while his captors were equipped with firearms.

Loaded with their prizes—both hostages and slaves—Stevens' party climbed up Bolivar Heights before beginning the long descent into lower town Harpers Ferry. Before sunup, the raiders arrived

Brown's force traveled along the canal towpath from the right of the image and across the Baltimore & Ohio Railroad bridge into Harpers Ferry. (hw)

outside the armory yard. To this moment, Lewis Washington was unconvinced of the serious intentions of his captors. But when the wagons approached the armory gate, "All's well," echoed from the front seat of the wagon. A military reply acknowledged the message and the entourage entered the armory yard, dispelling Washington's hopeful notions.

No moon illuminated Brown's march to Harpers Ferry on the night of October 16, 1859, though the landscape looked similar to this sketch of the town drawn in 1874. (loc)

John Brown was waiting in front of the engine house. The slaves, pikes in hand, immediately received orders to patrol the area. Brown, holding a Sharps rifle, approached John Allstadt and Lewis Washington. Brown had been warming himself around a small fire burning on the floor of the engine house, barely illuminating the bricks of the building's interior. He invited his prisoners to join him around the fire. Calm and composed, Brown informed his prisoners that he would attempt to get from their friends "a stout, able-bodied negro" and would in turn release the men from captivity. Turning to Washington, Brown cordially told him, "I wanted you particularly for the moral effect it would give our cause, having one of your name as a prisoner." Then, alluding to his goals for the raid, Brown muttered, "[T]his thing [slavery] must be put a stop to."

As calm and composed as Brown seemed, little did he know that the early momentum of his raid had begun to unravel.

On Sunday evening, before Brown's force reached the town, Patrick Higgins, a night watchman on the Baltimore & Ohio Railroad Bridge, and his wife passed across

These bridge piers carried both the Baltimore & Ohio and the Winchester & Potomac railroads, which passed through Harpers Ferry, across the Potomac River. Brown's men fired the first shots of the raid on this bridge. (loc)

the span from Harpers Ferry into Maryland to visit family. Higgins had crossed that bridge many times in his life, and upon crossing it once more that evening, he remembered, "Everything was as quiet as usual." Knowing his shift began in a few hours, Higgins ate dinner and went to bed.

Higgins overslept and failed to reach his post at the Maryland end of the bridge until 12:10 a.m. Odd, he thought, that the lanterns hanging from the bridge were out. Fortunately, Higgins had his own lamp in hand. He strode over to the time clock, a device that was to be pegged every half hour. The peg rested in the 10:30 p.m. slot, nearly two hours ago. Unsure of what all this meant, Higgins remained on the Maryland side for another twenty minutes, anticipating he would see his counterpart Bill Williams within that period. But Williams did not appear. Higgins held his lantern up near his head and began walking across the dark, one-thousand-foot-long covered bridge to investigate. How had this normal night become so abnormal?

Higgins then noticed two dark figures "armed with long spears" approaching from the Virginia side. One of them quietly asked Higgins, "Which way?" to which the watchman replied, "Not far; I am at my station." The reply was

Porte Crayon represented the hordes of civilians from Virginia and Maryland who grabbed their firearms and marched to Harpers Ferry to suppress Brown's Raid. (loc)

not the response these two men were looking for and they immediately grabbed him as a prisoner. Higgins swung at one of his captors, which allowed him to run free; he promptly headed for the nearest building, the Wager House Hotel.

Higgins' dash for the hotel was followed by two gunshots. One of the bullets grazed Higgins's head but the quick-thinking Irishman dashed to safety through one of the hotel windows. Inside he found hotel clerk W.W. Throckmorton, who had heard the gunshots. "Lock your doors," cried Higgins, "there are robbers on the bridge," as Throckmorton vainly searched for a revolver to defend himself. The peace Brown had hoped to maintain had instead flared into violence.

Despite his near-death encounter with the strangers prowling on the bridge, Higgins did not remain at the hotel. Instead, he walked to the nearby B&O depot to alert the baggageman and keeper of the depot, a former slave named Heyward Shepherd. Higgins's warning brought Shepherd into the growing and impromptu investigative team of Harpers Ferry citizens.

At about the same time, 1:25 a.m., a B&O express traveling from Wheeling to Baltimore chugged onto the tracks adjacent to the armory yard. Its conductor, Andrew Phelps, halted the train short of the railroad bridge, and noticed that no watchman stood his normal post there. After conferring with his crew

Phelps decided to steam across the span anyway. At this moment, Higgins "came up to me much excited," Phelps testified, "and stated that he had been attacked on the bridge by men having rifles." Alarmed, Phelps and several of his crew dismounted from the train and, led by lanterns, walked along the tracks to inspect. Heyward Shepherd joined the crew along the tracks.

An unscheduled early morning stop at Harpers Ferry made the train's passengers curious. "Every light in the town had been previously extinguished by the lawless mob," wrote one of them. "The train therefore remained stationary and the passengers, terribly affrighted, remained in the cars all night."

It did not take long for Phelps's team to reach the dark interior of the covered bridge. When they did, the words "stand and deliver" echoed down the roofed way and several gun barrels glinted off the lantern light. Phelps slowly backed out of the bridge to tell his engineer to reverse the train. Suddenly, the crack of a rifle shot broke the stillness. A staggering Heyward Shepherd exited the bridge and exclaimed to Phelps, "Captain, I am shot." Blood streamed from Shepherd's grievous wound as the bullet entered his back and exited just below his heart. A handful of men carried Shepherd back to the railroad office, where he shortly died. John Brown's Raid had claimed its first life, a free African American.

Amid the hysteria created by the mortal wounding of Shepherd, one of Brown's men departed his post on the railroad bridge and made for the armory gate. "There he goes now!" rang out a voice. An alarmed Throckmorton fired at the silhouette. His shot missed but two raiders near the armory gate leveled their weapons and replied to the hotel clerk. "[T]he reports were very loud, and I wondered why the people were not aroused," said Conductor Phelps.

Harpers Ferry's citizens may have slept soundly while Throckmorton dueled with the raiders but such was not the case for the train's passengers. The women and children passengers remained in the cars in a near panic, while some of the male passengers spilled into the streets of town. After Throckmorton's shootout with Brown's men, the clerk, conductor, and a host of passengers cautiously approached the armory yard. A

This image, similar to the 1859 sketch, was taken the year of Brown's attack on Harpers Ferry. The smokestack in the United States Armory, seen in the bottom center of the photograph, towered 90 feet above the armory yard below it. (loc)

few scattered shots fired from behind the gates greeted the group. Although no one was injured, the shots were close enough to prompt Throckmorton to open the Wager House Hotel for the train's passengers.

About this time, Stevens's parade of prisoners and slaves arrived at the armory. Dr. John Starry, a town resident who lived nearby, watched all of this transpire from his quarters. His curiosity getting the better of him, Starry visited the dying Shepherd before venturing out to determine the cause of all the commotion.

Starry planned to start with the armory watchman, Daniel Whelan. Instead, on reaching the armory gate he found himself on the wrong end of a carbine barrel. Stunned but stoic, Starry inquired where the watchman had gone. The voice behind the fence simply said he was not there, though there were "a few of us here.". With his questions unanswered, Starry returned to his home to keep an eye on these strange events.

Throckmorton and the train passengers likewise kept their gaze fixed on the armory yard. Brown allowed a prisoner to leave and go home as long as he passed along a message from Brown to the train operators. Brown wanted to let the train cross the bridge over the Potomac River. Suspicious and no doubt on edge, Phelps shot down the offer. He decided to wait "until daylight, that I might see whether it is safe."

Dr. John Starry served as a Paul Revere figure for Brown's Raid. He rode through the countryside alerting the locals to Brown's attack. (wvsa)

Before daybreak, at about 5:05 a.m., a wagon, guarded by a handful of armed men, departed the armory headed for Maryland. Starry witnessed this departure and decided Harpers Ferry needed assistance. He snuck from his home and alerted the local authorities and armory officials that an armed band of men had seized the armory. He warned them not to approach the armory yard. He next rode to neighboring Bolivar, where he "roused up some of the people." Perhaps unknowingly, Starry became the local leader working to oust the insurgents from the town.

As citizens gathered on the hill west of Harpers Ferry, Starry dispatched a network of riders to spread the alarm. Charlestown, Shepherdstown, and the Baltimore and Ohio Railroad company were put on notice of the trouble brewing at the confluence of the Shenandoah and Potomac Rivers. The doctor ordered the bells of St. John's Lutheran Church rung to wake those citizens still slumbering. But responses from those neighboring towns would take time. Starry began to take stock of what could be had on hand.

Judging from the "one or two squirrel rifles and a few shot guns" that Starry's minutemen brought to the table, his prospects for success looked dim. The armory workers who joined Starry's crew presented the dire news that all of the government's guns were in the arsenal, which the insurgents now controlled. Starry realized time was of the essence and mounted his horse. Leaving the gathering crowd of spectators and citizens overlooking the lower town of Harpers Ferry, Starry put spurs to his horse for Charlestown to hurry the local militia.

During their overnight capture of the armory and arsenal complex, Brown's men had seized various citizens that happened to walk past the armory or armory workers who showed up early for work. By the morning of October 17, Brown had between 30-40 prisoners in his custody around the engine house.

Brown treated his prisoners in an unexpected fashion. He did not hold them in the engine house, but instead allowed them to walk—under guard—through the armory yard. The raiders even allowed some hostages to return home to tell their families they were safe. At least one prisoner returned back to the armory.

The taking of hostages demonstrates another planning miscalculation by Brown—he did not have enough food to feed all his men plus his prisoners. Some of the prisoners' families visited to provide food. At dawn, Throckmorton at the Wager House Hotel received a note from Brown requesting breakfast for 45 men. The clerk fixed up what he could under the circumstances—coffee, rolls, and butter.

In 1859, the armory at Harpers Ferry stretched for 600 yards along the Potomac River and 20 buildings filled the yard. Today, the fire engine house is the only building still standing from this impressive factory.

Conductor Phelps was not yet a prisoner and he planned to keep it that way. Unsure of the raiders' intentions and worried for the safety of his passengers, Phelps determined to not move the train across the railroad bridge. However an early morning meeting with Brown calmed Phelps's nerves. "My head for it, you will not be hurt," Brown assured him. Brown called one more of his men to accompany them and, on foot, Brown, his raider, and Phelps preceded the train across the dark span. True to his word, Brown's presence allowed the train to pass the bridge's armed guards unharmed.

When the trio reached Maryland at approximately 6:30 a.m. Brown turned to Phelps and said, "You no doubt wonder that a man of my age should be here with a band of armed men, but if you knew my past history you would not wonder at it so much." Phelps bade the man (whom he only knew to be "Anderson") adieu, hopped on his train, and ordered his crew to steam away from Harpers Ferry as fast as possible.

At 7:05 a.m., Phelps's train reached Monocacy Junction, southeast of Frederick. Here he found the telegraph lines open and he scribbled off a note to be transmitted down the lines. "Express train bound east, under my charge, was stopped this morning at Harpers Ferry by armed abolitionists," the note began. "They are headed by a man who calls himself Anderson, and number about one hundred and fifty strong. They say they have come to free the slaves and intend to do it at all hazards." Phelps further stated that his was the last train the raiders would allow to pass through Harpers Ferry. "If it is attempted," he warned, "it will be at the peril of the lives of those having them in charge."

With this message, the world outside of the immediate vicinity of Harpers Ferry received its first news of John Brown's Raid. However, the recipient of Phelps's message scoffed at the absurdity of abolitionists stopping trains. "My dispatch was not exaggerated," Phelps retorted. "I have not made it half as bad as it is."

Simultaneous to Phelps's plea for help and Starry's ride to rouse the Charlestown militia, word was beginning to spread as the town slowly awoke. Starry's messages began the process. With daylight illuminating bedrooms and calling the town to wake up, more citizens learned of the nighttime affair.

The first man to arrive at the armory every morning was the bell ringer, James Darrell, whose ringing called the armory's workers to their stations to begin a day's work. But on this Monday, Darrell's bell hung silent. Near the armory gate, one of Brown's men had nabbed Darrell, though Brown, noting Darrell's age and health, released him.

Small groups of armory workers, drawn by habit rather than Darrell's bell, met a similar surprise when they approached the armory gate. Brown's sympathy was limited, however, and his stockpile of prisoners continued to grow.

Although Harpers Ferry's government armory sustained the town, not every citizen worked within its walls. While Brown's men were taking the early arrivals captive, Irishman Thomas Boerly walked down High Street to open his store for business. Shortly before 7:00 a.m., as Boerly descended from the high ground into the floodplain upon which Harpers Ferry sat, another townsman, Alexander Kelly, raced in the opposite direction. Kelly informed the large Irish storekeeper that several armed men had just unsuccessfully tried to capture him. Kelly and Boerly quickly returned to their homes to grab shotguns before they reunited again on High Street.

Now armed, the pair approached the corner of High and Shenandoah streets. Boerly spotted an African American man standing near the arsenal fence. He brought his shotgun to his shoulder and squeezed off an errant shot which had little effect except to draw return fire. One of those return shots hit Boerly's groin. He staggered for cover into a nearby shop where he soon bled out and died.

While John Starry rode for reinforcements, limited responses like Boerly's and Kelly's were all the townspeople could throw at Brown's force. Thus far, Brown's raid had disappointed his own hope to avoid bloodshed. However, he still controlled the most valuable commodity in town—guns. Citizens were enraged by Shepherd's and Boerly's deaths but, without a large cache of arms, there was little they could do to vent their anger at Brown's party.

Confusion about Brown's intentions, the strength of his forces, and even his identity helped shield the raiders from the townspeople. "[W]e had no idea how many there were," admitted Reverend Michael Costello, pastor of St. Peter's Catholic Church. "Of course we could do nothing just then." Unknown to Brown, nature, so often the enemy of the town and its occupants, would favor them in this desperate hour.

Brown's men controlled most of the guns in Harpers Ferry but not all the guns. Several weeks before the raid began, high waters endangered the stock of guns in the armory yard. Workers had moved them to higher ground in the stock house at the end of the armory, furthest from Brown's headquarters at the fire engine house.

The presence of these weapons was not unknown to the armory workers now locked out of work. Workers John McClelland and William Copeland got into this unguarded area. They grabbed bullet molds and percussion caps, then went next door to the stock house, where they obtained a number of serviceable firearms. The pair continued on until arriving at the powder house. Upon the men's return to Camp Hill, a prominence approximately one mile west of the lower town, Harpers Ferry's citizens had begun to stockpile their own arsenal of weapons.

In the lower town, Brown's forces remained at their positions at the armory, arsenal, and rifle factory along the Shenandoah River. One wagon, led by Charles Tidd and John Cook and flanked by William Leeman and five liberated slaves, departed Harpers Ferry for Maryland to bring weapons back from Kennedy Farm to Brown's force at the armory. Erratic fire from a handful of civilians forced Brown's men to take cover. Osborne Anderson remembered that on the morning of October 17, "we were prepared for commotion and tumult, but certainly not for more than we beheld around us." Brown's lieutenant in the rifle works, John Kagi, suggested to Brown that now was the time to vacate the town. Whether Brown ever received the proposal or he simply did not answer it is unknown. For now, Brown and his men remained.

The first organized resistance of local citizens to Brown's raiders formed on Camp Hill west of lower town, where in 1881 Anthony Hall was constructed as part of the Storer College campus. (kp)

Outside of Harpers Ferry, word began to spread. Near Charlestown, farmer James Hooff watched as his slaves planted a field. John Starry sprinted by on horseback, yelling that "whites and Negroes had possession of the Ferry & were killing citizens." Hooff, like others, grabbed his firearms and made haste to Charlestown. There, church bells rang, a clear indication of trouble on this Monday morning. In Shepherdstown, twelve miles up the Potomac River, Alexander Boteler was sitting down for breakfast when a carriage rolled up to his front door. His daughter quickly climbed down and yelled of recently received "startling intelligence of a negro insurrection at Harpers Ferry!"

News also arrived at Martinsburg, the seat of neighboring Berkeley County. The first reports were wildly exaggerated in the excitement of the moment.

"Armed abolitionists from the North—supposed to be some hundreds" according to one report, took possession of the town's gun factory and "were issuing guns to the negroes and shooting down unarmed citizens in the streets." The citizens were amazed at the stories, though that shock "soon gave place to an intense and pardonable indignation."

Wherever news of the raid reached, almost every citizen had the same reaction: grab arms and fight back. As Alexander Boteler rode through Shepherdstown on his way to Harpers Ferry, he noted the local militia company, the Hamtramck Guard, "was nearly ready to take up its line of march for the Ferry, while a goodly number of volunteers, with every sort of fire-arm, from old Tower muskets which had done service in colonial days to modern bird-guns, were joining them." Similar martial scenes were playing out in the streets of Charlestown and Martinsburg.

The stirring of militias and the general white population around Harpers Ferry did not go unnoticed by the slaves inhabiting the farms that dotted Jefferson County. This was a key element of Brown's plan—to draw in slaves from the countryside and arm them as members of his army. Some slaves had heard of the activity and what it meant through the "underground wires" and rushed to join the plot for their freedom, while others refused to join Brown's men.

The twenty-five to fifty slaves who joined Brown early in the raid had a myriad of reasons to do so. Some fought by Brown's side to help him achieve his goal, which was ultimately their goal, too. Others came to Harpers Ferry because the raiders forced them to. Such was the case for four of Lewis Washington's slaves and six of John Allstadt's. Most performed tasks supportive of the raiders. However, when Brown's— and their—prospects of success began to fade, many attempted to flee and plead innocence.

Even still, the majority of the local enslaved population did not actively participate in the raid. While the "underground wires" flowed from one slave community to another with information about the excitement at Harpers Ferry, the slaves cheerfully acknowledged the news but, rather than risk fleeing, waited for news from the Ferry. Rather than slaves fleeing to Brown's banner, by mid-morning on October 17, it was mostly armed white militia.

"A More Dismal Night Cannot Be Imagined"

Harpers Ferry, A Scene of War

CHAPTER FIVE

OCTOBER 17, 1859, MORNING -
OCTOBER 17, 1859, NIGHT

John Brown's Fort, situated today a few dozen yards from where it originally stood, has been moved four times. The building is missing its bell, which Company I, 13th Massachusetts Infantry took in 1861. The bell is today displayed in Marlborough, Massachusetts. (kp)

Grasping the gravity of the situation, one hundred men of the Jefferson Guards formed into two companies on the streets of Charlestown. After quickly electing officers, the men marched to the nearby rail depot, bound for the seat of war. After a short train ride to Halltown, halfway between Charlestown and Harpers Ferry, the militia detrained so the engine could travel to Winchester and bring more reinforcements. The Guards commander, Robert W. Baylor, also called on nearby Shepherdstown for support.

The Charlestown militia continued on foot towards Harpers Ferry. Rumors abounded along their route of march. Raiders had ripped up the railroad tracks into town, said one, which proved to be false. When Baylor's men reached Camp Hill, where the town's citizens had gathered to monitor the raiders, Baylor found the crowd "in very great excitement." Though not heavily armed, the citizens were preparing to fight back. Women and children took items from their homes to melt for bullets, using the molds confiscated earlier by John McClelland and William Copeland. "Father and the others

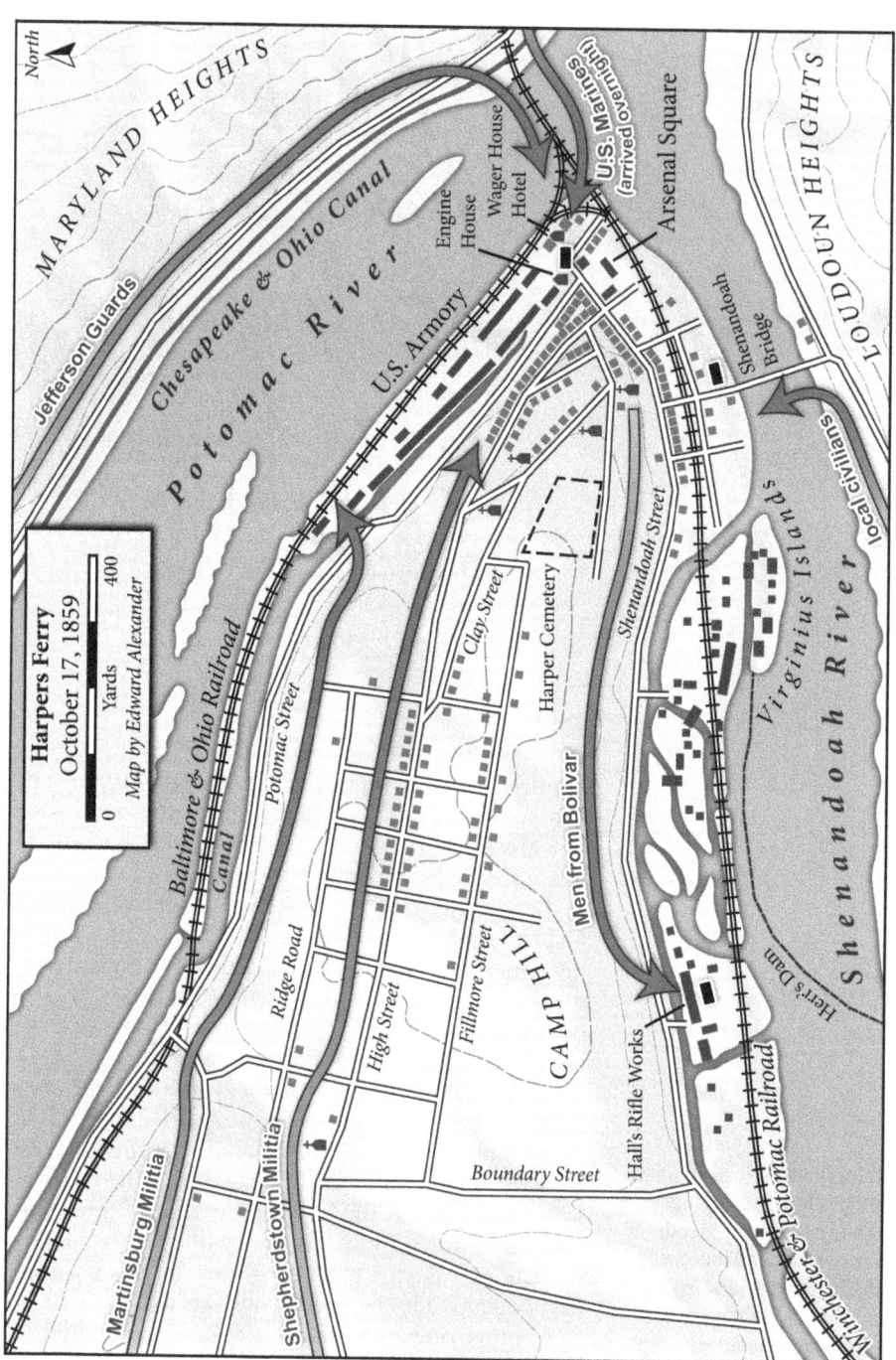

Harpers Ferry
October 17, 1859

0   Yards   400

Map by Edward Alexander

were putting bullets into their pockets, hot from the moulds," remembered fifteen-year-old Jennie Chambers. Ready to work with what he had, Baylor recruited these armed citizens into two additional companies of militia.

As Baylor's force prepared for the task at hand, John Brown contemplated his next move. The staff of the Wager House Hotel had delivered breakfast for him, his men, and their prisoners. However, few ate it, fearing that the food was poisoned. On October 17, "John Brown and most of his men fought without a morsel to eat," wrote Oswald Villard, an early Brown biographer. Brown either disregarded or never received John Kagi's order to immediately leave Harpers Ferry. Regardless, Brown initiated negotiations with Harpers Ferry's citizens from, as he thought, a position of strength.

The terms of Brown's proposal stated that the citizens would cease their haphazard firing on Brown and his men, especially at the armory, and leave him in possession of his current holdings. Prisoner Joseph Brua served as an intermediary between Brown and the angry townspeople "begging the citizens not to shoot." Brua's pleas fell on deaf ears as scattered shots split the air in the lower town.

The corner of Shenandoah and High Street (center) was a deadly place to stand from October 16-18, 1859. (kp)

Before noon, shortly after reaching Camp Hill, Baylor's militia prepared to ensnare Brown's force. Baylor ordered Captain John Rowan's Jefferson Guards to cross the Potomac River upstream from Harpers Ferry and take possession of the railroad bridge from the Maryland side, thus cutting off Brown's escape route into that state. Baylor split the citizens into two companies. He ordered one company under the command of Captain Lawson Botts to seize the bridge spanning the Shenandoah River before taking positions around the Gault House, a hotel and saloon near the Baltimore and Ohio rail depot. Baylor tasked the other company, under Captain John Avis, "to take possession of the houses directly in front of the Arsenal." Baylor dispatched his three captains from his council and orders snapped atop Camp Hill. Men grabbed their arms as Baylor's three-pronged approach began.

Rain fell as the militia began their march. Rowan, a Mexican War veteran, and his Jefferson Guards had received the most ambitious task. His command marched north from Camp Hill to the banks of the Potomac River, approximately one mile upstream from the armory yard. Rowan's men utilized a small fleet of flatboats to cross the river—shrouded in mist—to flank Brown's force from the Maryland side. The crossing succeeded without any problems.

As Rowan's men cautiously trod downstream on the towpath of the Chesapeake and Ohio Canal, the rainy conditions in the river valley fogged their vision. Fortunately for the Jefferson Guards, the conditions similarly affected the visibility for Brown's men in the armory and those guarding the Maryland end of the railroad bridge. At noon, the Guards came within range of the bridgehead. "Every man felt when he reached the Maryland end of the Potomac Bridge that he had literally 'run the gauntlet,' and we were all glad to be alive," recalled one of Rowan's men.

Oliver Brown and two other raiders guarded the B&O bridge, Brown's lifeline to Maryland and points north. All was quiet until Rowan's nearly two dozen men charged out of the mist and quickly drove the defenders back across the river and into Harpers Ferry. Both sides exchanged a brief but "smart firing" for possession of the bridge. When the smoke settled, Rowan's Jefferson Guards had cut Brown's link to Maryland, his reinforcements, and his stockpile of arms at the schoolhouse armory. Brown's three defenders—his son Oliver, Stewart Taylor, and Dangerfield Newby—dashed for the cover of the armory and arsenal buildings.

In town, the situation was quickly deteriorating for Brown's men. Lawson Botts, tasked with seizing the Shenandoah bridge, led his command past Jefferson's Rock and downhill to the river floodplain. Botts left a detachment to hold the crossing while the rest of his command took positions in the Gault House Saloon, overlooking the rear of the arsenal grounds.

Captain John Avis's company went straight at Brown's shrinking defensive perimeter in Arsenal Square and the lower end of the armory yard. All three prongs of the attack converged almost simultaneously shortly after noon. When Avis and his men moved down High Street in the direction of the arsenal

buildings, Oliver Brown and his two companions at the bridge were racing back to the armory. The rapid fluidity of the situation caught men in the open. Shots again rang out between both sides.

George W. Turner had joined Avis's company only moments earlier. Turner, a native Virginian, graduated eighth in the United States Military Academy's Class of 1831. His classmates included future Union generals Samuel Curtis and Andrew Humphreys. After graduation, Turner remained at West Point to teach mathematics before being stationed in South Carolina during the Nullification Crisis. Turner served in various other posts until he resigned his commission in 1836. Since then, he peacefully farmed a plot of land near Charlestown and for a short time oversaw the town's academy. He "had the respect and esteem of the entire community."

Earlier that morning, word arrived at Turner's home that his friend, Colonel Lewis Washington, was the prisoner of "a band of ruffians" headquartered in Harpers Ferry. Turner immediately mounted his horse and rode to the town. Someone handed Turner a shotgun as he walked down High Street amid Avis's men.

As Avis and his men approached the corner of High and Shenandoah streets, scattered shots erupted from the armory and arsenal yards. One bullet struck Turner in the left shoulder, collapsing him instantly

High Street became an avenue of advance for Harpers Ferry's citizens looking to take potshots at Brown's men and then for the Shepherdstown militia during its attack on October 17. (kp)

Hogs rooted through Dangerfield Newby's remains in an alleyway gruesomely immortalized today as Hog Alley.
(kp)

only yards from the intersection. He did not linger long before dying.

Avis's force, aided by locals who had perched themselves around the lower town, now stormed toward the arsenal. Avis himself grabbed a firearm from the hands of Leonard Sadler, a War of 1812 veteran who sought one more fight. With musket in hand, Avis pounded the door of one of the arsenal buildings until it opened. His company managed to secure the yard but not the buildings themselves.

Baylor's plan had succeeded brilliantly, but the death of Turner left the citizens and militia enraged. Brown's fleeing men, caught in the open, provided excellent targets upon which they could vent their anger and fear. One of Brown's men, former slave Dangerfield Newby, became one of those targets.

The militia's swift attack drove Brown's men from the covered bridge and the two arsenal buildings as they fled for the safety of the engine house near the gate of the armory yard. One Harpers Ferry citizen took aim at the fleeing raiders from the upper story of a building at the corner of Shenandoah and High streets. Apparently not all of the citizens received the benefit of the bullet moulds, as this civilian loaded a "six-inch iron spike" down the muzzle of his gun and aimed it at Newby, who was defiantly firing during his retrograde movement to the engine house. The perched shooter squeezed the trigger. In an instant, Newby fell, mortally wounded.

Newby lay in the street, clinging to life, which quickly flowed from his body through a gaping wound to the neck. "I never saw, on any battle-field, a more hideous musket-wound than his," remembered a former Confederate soldier years after Brown's Raid, the spike having cut his throat "literally from ear to ear." Another witness to Newby's death wrote that his neck wound was "gaping open quite large enough to admit the fore part of an ordinary sized foot." Newby quickly perished from his wound.

Despite his death, the town's citizens were not finished with Newby's remains. Someone carved the ears off Newby's head as a memento of the history unfolding in Harpers Ferry. Hogs rooted the corpse, too. Occasionally, bullets fired from drunk or vengeful citizens pocked the dead man's remains still lying in the street. Newby was Brown's first casualty, though far from his last. For his companions that saw the way citizens treated Newby's remains, it no doubt cast a shadow over their early successes.

Baylor's coordinated attack had shrunk Brown's possessions in Harpers Ferry from a sizable portion of the town to just three small areas—the lower armory yard, the arsenal buildings, and Hall's Rifle Works along the Shenandoah River. But worse for Brown, with the bridges lost, his escape routes out of Harpers Ferry were no longer viable options.

Across the river that morning, the force of Cook, Tidd, Leeman, and five liberated slaves attempted to achieve their mission of bringing weapons from the Kennedy Farm to Brown's raiders and also to free slaves and imprison their masters. The mission began successfully enough as the small crew captured local man Terence Byrne but failed to free his slaves who were not present at Byrne's home. Leeman brought Byrne to Harpers Ferry after he, Cook, and Tidd confiscated a small schoolhouse for use as their forward arsenal. This appropriation occurred peaceably. Cook allowed the school's students to go home but "detained" teacher Lind Currie. As the two discussed "the feeling entertained towards the south by the north generally," the sound of fire grew from Harpers Ferry. Currie

This street sign is the only reminder of the grim history that happened in Hog Alley. (kp)

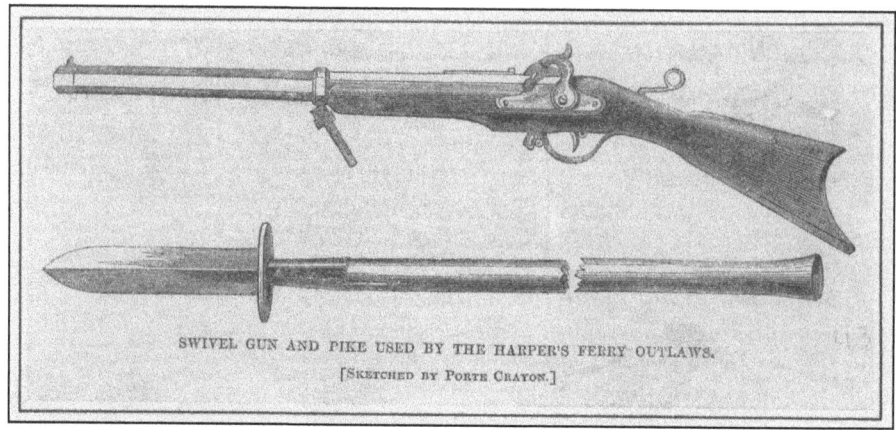

SWIVEL GUN AND PIKE USED BY THE HARPER'S FERRY OUTLAWS.
[Sketched by Porte Crayon.]

Brown's plan called for storing weapons, such as firearms and pikes. (nypl)

asked Cook the meaning of the gunfire, to which Cook coldly replied, "well, it simply means that those people down there are resisting our men, and we are shooting them down."

Citizens turned sharpshooters kept Brown's positions warm for the insurgents. The constant fire forced Brown and his men stationed in the armory yard to fully retreat into the engine house. They confined eleven prisoners there with them while Brown placed the rest in the adjacent watchman's room. Hemmed within the building, Brown began to fortify his position. He directed one of the Allstadt's slaves to drill holes in the engine house's stout wooden doors so Brown's men could return the fire raining on them from multiple directions.

Brown's demeanor remained calm as his situation dimmed. However, he was not oblivious to the fact that some drastic changes to his plans must take place in order for his raid to be successful. He would try resorting to less violent measures to get the situation back under his control.

As bullets crashed through the windows of the engine house and turned its bricks into dust, Brown called raider William Thompson and a prisoner named Cross to his side. Cross agreed, under Thompson's escort, to broker a ceasefire. Once the measure caught the attention of the citizen shooters and quieted their arms, Cross and Thompson left the armory yard and walked to the nearby Wager House Hotel. Near the hotel, angry citizens pounced on Thompson, hauled him inside, and tied him to a chair for questioning. Interrogators demanded to know the meaning of all of this—why had Brown's men attacked Harpers Ferry? Thompson stated he personally believed slaves "were cruelly treated and would gladly avail themselves of the first opportunity to obtain their freedom." Thus, he and his companions believed when word of their successful operations reached the countryside, "the colored people would come in a mass, backed by the non-slaveholders of the Valley of Virginia." Thompson's comments no doubt further enraged the crowd within earshot of the interrogation and confirmed their worst fears—Brown's band was attempting to foment a slave uprising.

Undeterred by his first failed attempt at negotiation, Brown dispatched a second party to plead for terms. This group consisted of Aaron Stevens, Brown's son Watson, and prisoner Archibald Kitzmiller, the armory's acting superintendent. Earlier in the day, Kitzmiller had "made repeated efforts to accommodate matters with Brown," he testified later. His efforts had been fruitless, but with his force hemmed in, Brown gave the angered Kitzmiller his chance.

The trio ventured out from the engine house to diplomatically move the militia off the bridge into Maryland. Kitzmiller fluttered his handkerchief to signal a cease fire before the three men departed the safety of the building. "If the citizens understood what the flag [handkerchief] meant, they did not respect it," Brown biographer Oswald Villard wrote. Immediately after the three emissaries exited the armory yard, the local militias began firing at them. A shot fired from the Gault House struck Stevens, who swore and returned fire. Next to him, Watson Brown fell as shots continued to pelt the trio. Stevens ultimately suffered six wounds in the exchange. "I have been cruelly deceived," yelled the wounded raider to Kitzmiller. The acting superintendent simply replied, "I wish I had remained at home."

Watson Brown staggered back to the engine house, bleeding from a gaping stomach wound. Another round of failed negotiations and the sight of his son laying in a pool of blood was the tipping point for John Brown. He turned to his prisoners huddled in the engine room and exclaimed "he had it in his power to destroy that place in half an hour, but would not do it, unless resisted."

Aaron Stevens could not muster enough strength to reach safety. Instead he laid in a street gutter, bleeding from his multiple wounds. "I seen big beefs killed and they did not lose more blood," remembered a witness to Stevens's wounding. Stevens was "a

large, exceedingly athletic man, a perfect Samson in appearance" and would not die that easily as he stumbled in attempts to reach the engine house.

Though Brown could risk no more of his men to attempt a rescue of Stevens, hostage Joseph Brua volunteered to aid the wounded man. Brua had earlier tried to broker a ceasefire. Now he ventured out of the engine house and carried Stevens's large, wounded form into a bed in the Wager House Hotel, before returning to the engine house to resume his place as a prisoner.

About the same time as Kitzmiller's failed peace entreaty, raider William Leeman, the youngest of Brown's men, believed the situation at Harpers Ferry was hopeless and determined to escape anyway he could. Using Kitzmiller's mission as the needed diversion, Leeman slipped away through the armory, ducking as he ran to avoid notice. He plunged into the Potomac River at a shallow point upstream from the railroad bridge. The water fought him, and Leeman struggled to move quickly. Soon, gunmen on the bridge noticed the lone raider and began to shoot at him. Bullets sprayed water in Leeman's face. Realizing the hopelessness of his situation, Leeman reached a small spit of land in the river and threw up his hands in frustration, pleading, "Don't shoot!"

Citizen George Schoppert splashed into the Potomac River, and on reaching Leeman thrust his gun at point blank range into the young man's face. Schoppert, later claiming Leeman was armed with a pistol and knife, pulled the trigger. Leeman was instantly killed. Schoppert rifled through Leeman's pockets and left his body lying in the river. As the bars of the Gault and Wager houses continued to pour liquor for the militia and citizens through the afternoon, the increasingly angry and intoxicated crowd would use his corpse for target practice.

*   *   *

The situation of Brown's raiders continued to deteriorate rapidly. Brown had previously dispatched John Kagi, Lewis Leary, and John Copeland to the rifle works on Hall's Island along the Shenandoah River. They were joined by two local slaves. When Dr. John Starry saw a crowd of citizens looking for action, he suggested, "if they wanted to show their bravery," they could do so by attacking the rifle works. The citizens moved up the Shenandoah towards Kagi's position.

By 2:30 p.m., Starry had organized a force of locals and placed it "under the command of a young man named Irwin," the doctor later testified. Irwin's scratch force lined the bluff west of Jefferson's Rock and poured a hot fire into the workshops where Kagi and his men sheltered. "Hungry, isolated and menaced by more and more armed men," Kagi prepared for a fight, but it turned out his small force didn't have much "fight" in it. Irwin's first volley sent the three raiders and a slave named Jim, who drowned in the attempt, rushing from the rifle factory and into the Shenandoah River.

Ben, a slave of John Allstadt who took up arms because "if he didn't keep guard at [the] Rifle factory they would kill him," ran towards, rather than away from, the assailants. Reverend Charles White questioned the slave but ultimately believed his innocence. Others in the crowd pointed their guns at him to, as they said, deal out justice. White stepped

The raiders who occupied the rifle works on Hall's Island fled across the Shenandoah River below Jefferson's Rock, seen at right. (loc)

between the armed men and Ben and prevented him from being shot. Unfortunately, Ben only lived eight more days, dying of "Pneumonia & fright" in a Charlestown jail cell. His mother, who cared for him in the jail, died the following month.

The rest of Kagi's force managed to make it to the riverbank unscathed. "The river at that point runs rippling over a rocky bed, and at ordinary stages of the water is easily forded," said Alexander Boteler, an eyewitness to the attack on the rifle works. Kagi, Leary, and Copeland rushed into the river and, slowed by its current, made their attempt at escape. Another group of armed citizens under the command of Captain Henry Medler held positions on the far side of the river opposite the rifle factory. To this point, Medler's crew had had little to do. All of that quickly changed.

Medler's command contested Kagi's crossing. Water shoots splashed around the escapees as bullets missed their mark. More than halfway across the Shenandoah, Kagi received a bullet to the head, his body sinking beneath the water. The "fire of at leas [sic] fifty men was then turned upon poor Leary and myself," Copeland wrote. Leary relented. Soaking wet, he crawled onto a large rock in the middle of the river and turned to look back at the trailing Copeland. Suddenly, Leary crumpled under the impact of a bullet to his back. He would remain on that rock for ten hours before succumbing to his wounds.

Copeland's odds did not look favorable. He floated down the river to another large rock outcropping, crouching close behind it. He hoped that by waiting out the crowd, they might believe he was dead. Like with William Leeman, the citizens were hardly content to allow a raider to escape—they were out for blood.

James Holt and a host of armed men waded out into the Shenandoah River towards the rock where Leary lay. In the process, they surprisingly discovered Copeland in his hidden crevice. Holt pulled his pistol and pointed it at Copeland, with Copeland following suit. Both men squeezed their triggers, but the spark from the hammers striking the cap met only wet powder and neither gun discharged. Holt moved closer to Copeland as the river's current carried him downstream. Each passing second brought the two combatants within closer range. But each time they tried to fire; no shots followed. By this point, Copeland climbed the rock that he had been clinging to. Holt reached it, ascended out of the river, and prepared to club the raider to death with his pistol. Copeland threw his gun into the river and raised his hands in submission.

"Lynch him!" yelled the crowd of onlookers when Copeland came ashore. These cries for his painful death "badly frightened" the prisoner. Holt and his band walked along the shore of the Shenandoah downstream to the epicenter of the action near the junction of the two rivers. Citizens began to carry through on their threat, creating an ever longer rope of handkerchiefs with which to hang the man. Fortunately for Copeland, John Starry wheeled his horse to the scene and shielded Copeland until a militia officer arrived and hurried the prisoner to safety.

Throughout the day, Heyward Shepherd—the first casualty of Brown's Raid—had clung to life. About 3:00 p.m., Shepherd could fight no more and died in the B&O Railroad office. Disturbed most by this loss was Harpers Ferry's mayor and a well-respected citizen throughout Jefferson County, Fontaine Beckham.

Beckham and Shepherd had a unique relationship. Virginia law required Shepherd, a free black man, to have a white sponsor in order to remain and work in Harpers Ferry while living in a neighboring county. For the decade or so before Shepherd's death, Beckham had vouched for Shepherd.

Mayor Beckham became "greatly excited" when Shepherd died. Throughout the day's events, a despondent Beckham remained in the room while Shepherd slowly declined. Shepherd's death prompted Beckham, despite the urging of others, to walk along the railroad tracks in the direction of the armory to view what was transpiring. He did not travel far amid the whiz of bullets before indignant citizens pulled him back to safety. But soon, lantern in hand, he ventured out again. It is debated whether or not Beckham also carried a pistol in his coat pocket.

This time, Beckham made it to the base of the water pump placed in the northeast corner of the armory. Using the pump as his shield, Beckham leaned around it several times to take a good look at Brown's engine house fortress. Men on both sides were becoming increasingly jittery as violence and casualties mounted.

Beckham had not been the first to use the water pump for cover. Brown's men kept a close eye on this pump. They were aware of the dangers lurking there after earlier shots fired from the pump hit the engine house walls. Edwin Coppoc, peering through one of the firing holes bored through the building's heavy wooden doors, saw Beckham poke his head from behind the tank, go behind it for cover, and then pop his head out again. "If he keeps on peeking, I'm going to shoot," he muttered. The dodging head appeared again and Coppoc's rifle cracked. Coppoc's shot whizzed harmlessly past the pump. Prisoners urged Coppoc, "Don't fire, man, for God's sake! They'll shoot in here and kill us all." Instead Coppoc again leveled his firearm, aimed at the familiar spot where the bobbing head would soon reappear, and waited.

Bang! Coppoc's second shot whirled in the pump's direction. This time, it found its mark, striking Beckham in the heart. The mayor toppled instantly onto the tracks. He quickly expired but his exposed location prevented friends from retrieving his body, despite repeated attempts.

Many citizens heard the bullet that struck Beckham whistle through the air and saw him fall hard to the ground. One of the witnesses was Henry Hunter, Beckham's grandnephew. Hunter spent the earlier part of the day "fighting on my own hook," he testified. He became "much exasperated" at the mayor's death, as did all those who witnessed it, and decided to seek revenge.

Hunter and George Chambers, followed by a crowd, stormed into the Wager House Hotel room where William Thompson sat in a chair with his hands tied behind him. Hunter and Chambers, the two leaders of the rabble, pointed their guns at the prisoner. Before they could fire, Christine Fouke, whose brother operated the hotel, threw herself between the gun muzzles and a helpless Thompson.

Her action was not out of pity for Thompson. She called Beckham's death a "cold-blooded murder" just like the rest. Instead, she did not want the floors and walls stained with Thompson's blood, "however much he deserved to die." Additionally, "I am emphatically a law and order woman," she wrote, "and wanted the self-condemned man to live, that he might be disposed of by the law." Fouke got half her wish. Hunter grabbed Thompson by the throat and dragged him out to the railroad bridge. Thompson, between struggling for air with Hunter's hand clasped around his neck,

The railroad lantern carried by Fontaine Beckham at the time of his death—etched with the initials "F. B."—has been passed down by generations of Beckham descendants. (jeg)

warned, "Though you may take my life, 80,000 will rise up to avenge me, and carry out my purpose of giving liberty to the slaves."

Thompson was executed on the bridge, "a dozen or more balls were buried in him," noted an eyewitness. The crowd tossed Thompson's body into the river below. Still angry for blood, Hunter's and Chambers's crew returned to the Wager House Hotel to end Aaron Stevens's misery. However, his wounds seemed dire and serious enough that "we concluded to spare him, and start after others, and shoot all we could find." Hunter justified his actions in court, believing that his beloved uncle's death justified his violent response. "I felt it my duty, and I have no regrets."

St. Peter's Catholic Church, perched above the lower town near Jefferson's Rock, was rebuilt in 1896, and today serves as a chapel with regular Mass for Harpers Ferry residents and tourists. (jeg)

*   *   *

Soon more militia reached Harpers Ferry from Shepherdstown and Martinsburg, the two companies reaching the hill above Harpers Ferry simultaneously. Colonel Baylor greeted the new arrivals and ordered the Shepherdstown company to continue along the main road into the town below and enter the armory yard at the main gate. While the Shepherdstown company's movements distracted the raiders, Ephraim G. Alburtis would lead several dozen of his Martinsburg militia into the far end of the armory yard to hit Brown's force from the other direction.

Once in position, Alburtis divided his own force into three columns. Alburtis himself led the main column of 25 men down the roadway through the center of the armory yard while two other contingents of roughly equal size worked their way towards the engine house using the shop buildings to leapfrog towards their objective.

Alburtis's force inched closer to the engine house in the lower end of the yard. When the militia were just a few buildings away, the rifle fire, which had alternately slackened and increased throughout the day, reached a fever pitch. Brown's men in the engine house and posted outside the armory gate opened fire into the advancing militia companies, stunning both. A few of the Martinsburg men fell in the fire.

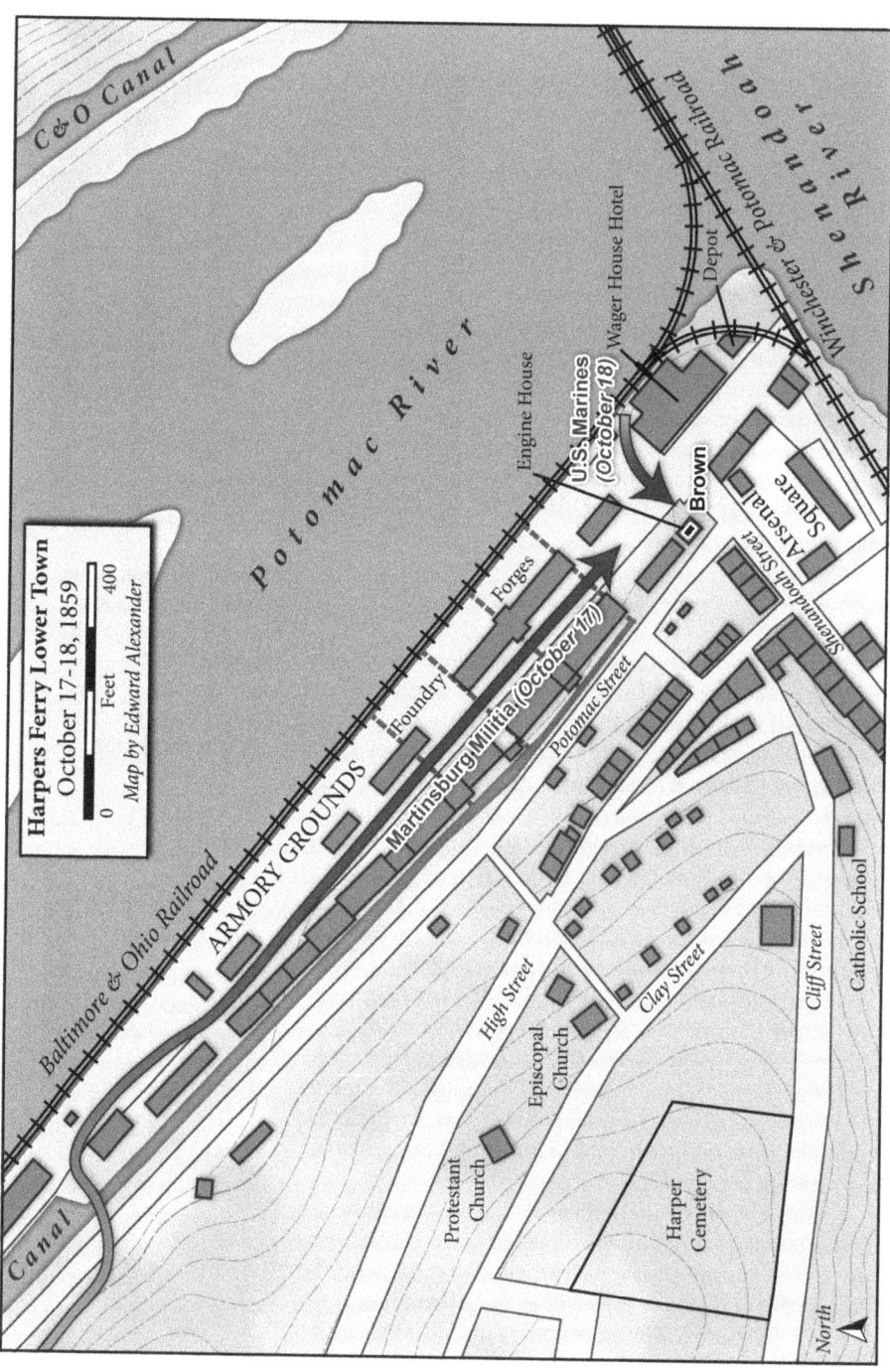

Harpers Ferry Lower Town
October 17-18, 1859
Map by Edward Alexander

"[P]oorly armed, some with pistols and others with shot-guns," Alburtis's force replied to Brown's Sharps carbines however they could.

Across the river, John Cook departed his position at the schoolhouse armory to get a look at the situation in Harpers Ferry. The crackle of rifle fire grew in intensity as he neared the town. Hoping to gain a better vantage point, Cook scaled Maryland Heights. From the side of the hill, he saw his comrades "completely surrounded" and under fire. "I thought I would draw their fire upon myself," Cook said later. Cook climbed a tree, raised his rifle, aimed and, from a half-mile away, fired on the advancing militia. The gunsmoke exploding with each shot betrayed Cook's position. Some of Alburtis's men and other armed citizens turned their attention and guns on the lone sharpshooter. It took several attempts but the final shot sent up the mountain clipped a limb Cook used for support and sent him tumbling fifteen feet to the ground. He landed hard. "I was severely bruised and my flesh somewhat lacerated," he admitted. Having suffered enough, Cook began his escape.

Brown's men selected this one room schoolhouse, no longer standing, as their forward armory for the raid. (WVSA)

Despite the intense fire from Cook and Brown's men, about 20 of the Martinsburg militiamen surged towards the engine house, spurred on by railroad worker George Wollet. In order to fire their rifles, Brown's men kept the large doors of the engine house open three to five inches. Wollet took advantage of this opportunity and began to push the doors open. But before he could cross the threshold of the engine house, Wollet's heroics were ended by a bullet to the arm.

The Martinsburg contingent now discovered the placement of most of Brown's hostages in the watchman's room. Unable to breach the main room of the building, which Brown and his most prominent prisoners occupied, the Martinsburg men smashed the windows of the side chamber and succeeded in freeing thirty to forty prisoners.

Alburtis's quick attack drew intense rifle fire from Brown's men. The Martinsburg men counted eight wounded, two of whom suffered serious wounds. But the militia gave as good as they got, mortally wounding raiders Stewart Taylor and Brown's son Oliver, both of whom fell inside the engine house.

While this late afternoon militia attack further constricted Brown's hold in Harpers Ferry and confined him to the engine house, Alburtis believed more might have been accomplished. "We could have ended the business," he reported, had the other companies supported him.

In the face of his situation, Brown still believed he could negotiate from a position of strength. He sent prisoner Isaac Russell as an emissary to Baylor. Brown sought a truce, whereby his force would leave Harpers Ferry and, once in Maryland, would release the hostages. Baylor could not accept those terms. The colonel drafted his rebuttal and enlisted Samuel Strider to carry the message to Brown. Strider fixed a handkerchief to his umbrella—the rain continuing to fall—and strode to the engine house. Brown opened Baylor's note and read, in part: "if you will set at liberty our citizens, we will leave the government to deal with you concerning their property as it may think most advisable."

Brown was not satisfied. He quickly penned a rebuttal and handed it back to Strider. Brown believed all of his men, those across the Potomac River and Maryland and those he did not realize had been killed, would soon join him. Thus reinforced, he would leave the town, cross the river into Maryland, and release the prisoners there. Only after this head start would Brown negotiate with the government. Upon receiving this last note, Baylor finally ended the diplomacy. "The terms you proposed I cannot accept," he wrote. "Under no consideration will I consent to a removal of our citizens across the river. The only negotiations upon which I will consent to treat are those which have been previously proposed to you." The initiative rested in Baylor's hands. Now that he called off negotiations after Brown declined the latest terms, Brown's men had little to do but wait and see what the morning brought.

All day, as the sounds of combat occasionally echoed up the Potomac River Valley, Cook and Tidd at the schoolhouse armory and Owen Brown, Barclay Coppoc, and Francis Meriam at the Kennedy farm contemplated their next move.

After retreating from the Maryland hillside from where he engaged the Virginia militia, Cook headed back towards the Kennedy farmhouse. On the way there, he encountered Brown, Coppoc, Meriam, and Tidd. The group weighed their options. Owen Brown opposed returning to Harpers Ferry. Tidd was adamant that they must escape. Brown later recalled Tidd's pleading, "The fact is, boys, we are used up; the best thing we can do is to get away from here as quick as we can." They deemed it "sheer madness" to try and break the militia's encirclement of Brown's Harpers Ferry position. On the night of October 17, the five men convened at the Kennedy farm. Fearful that one of Allstadt's slaves, who had fled their grasp to return to Virginia, might betray their location, the men decided they must leave immediately. The five men abandoned Brown's mission, left the farmhouse, and traveled cross-country over hill and valley.

Darkness quickly settled over the unimaginable scenes in Harpers Ferry. Word reached the militia that more volunteers from Virginia and Maryland, and a force of professional soldiers, were en route. Baylor recognized that the darkness would only add to the confusion and add unnecessarily to the casualty toll. He called off all operations for the night. Militiamen took their posts around Brown's small sphere of occupation in the lower armory yard to prevent any attempts at escape.

Though the violence temporarily halted, the night of October 17 was not entirely peaceful. "The atmosphere was raw and cold," recorded citizen Joseph Barry. Harpers Ferry's men and women replayed in their minds the grisly events of that day and the deaths of their own townsfolk. The raiders' bodies lay in the streets where they fell. Increasingly intoxicated militiamen pocked Thompson's and Leeman's remains full of lead, while others prodded Newby's corpse with sticks. "Now, a cloudy and moonless sky hung like a pall over the scene of war," Barry continued, "and, on the whole, a more dismal night cannot be imagined." The events of October 17 would have been unimaginable to its citizens even a day ago.

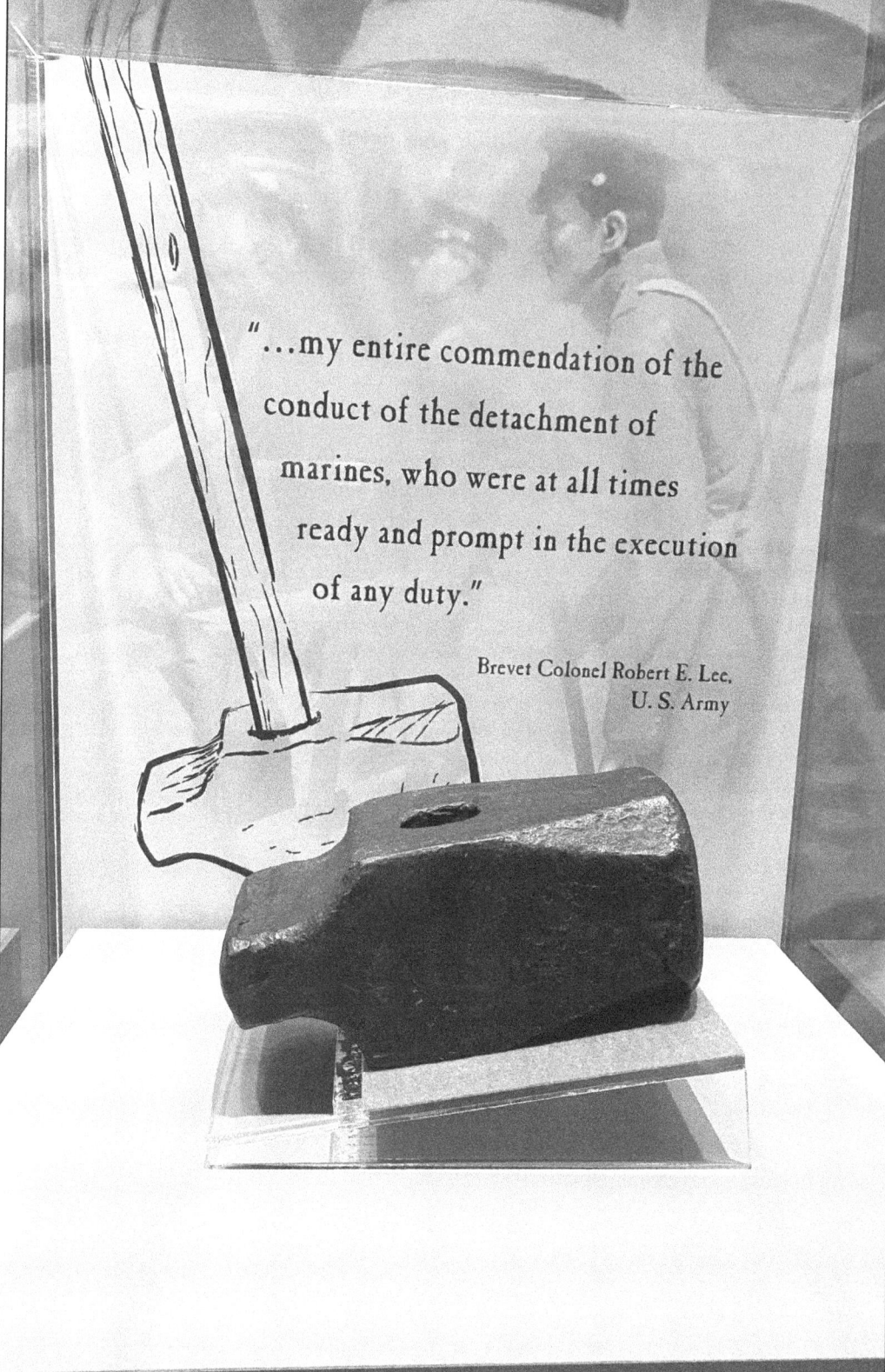

"The Whole Was Over in a Few Minutes"

John Brown's Raid Suppressed

CHAPTER SIX

OCTOBER 17, 1859, NIGHT - OCTOBER 19, 1859

The head of one of the sledgehammers used to break into John Brown's fort is on display at the United States Marine Corps Museum in Quantico, Virginia. (cm)

The occupants of Arlington House rose on the morning of October 17, 1859, as if it were any other Monday. The sunrise revealed their splendid view of the nation's capital, punctuated by the unfinished monument to its founding father George Washington and the pulleys and cranes festooned atop the Capitol building to install its new dome. Washington City was, much like the nation it symbolized, an unfinished product.

Two men who arose early in Arlington House were witnesses to the nation's expansion but were also well aware of its fissures and cracks that occasionally caused trouble for the United States. Lieutenant Colonel Robert E. Lee was in his third decade of active military service to his country while Lieutenant James Ewell Brown "J. E. B." Stuart had less than one decade under his belt. Despite the age disparity, both men were well acquainted with one another, Lee having invited Stuart to stay at Arlington House while the young lieutenant was in Washington on personal business. Early that morning, both descended from Arlington House's prominent hill. Stuart was headed for Washington and Lee for neighboring Alexandria.

J. E. B. Stuart visited the United States War Department at Pennsylvania Avenue and 17th Street to arrange the details of his new contract with the Federal government over his recently approved patent for a mechanism that made it easier for mounted cavalrymen to detach their sabers from their belts.

Upon Stuart's arrival, he sensed a quiet tension in the building. Whispers spoke of a disturbance seventy miles up the Potomac River at Harpers Ferry. Secretary of War John B. Floyd attempted to hush the rumors "for fear of a rise at Washington," Stuart recalled. While in the War Department, Stuart "accidentally," in his own words, heard the report. "[A]lthough scarcely anything was known except that the Harpers Ferry armory was in the possession of a mob of rumor said over 3000 men, still it was pretty generally surmised that it was a servile insurrection," the lieutenant wrote.

The first report that reached Washington of any trouble in Harpers Ferry stemmed from Conductor Phelps's first message sent from Monocacy Junction. John W. Garrett, the Baltimore and Ohio Railroad's President, dispersed the information to the Maryland militia, Virginia governor Henry Wise, United States Secretary of War John B. Floyd, and, at 10:30 a.m., President James Buchanan. "The presence of United States troops is indispensable, for the safety of Government property and of the mails," Garrett told the President.

This simple monument marks the original location of the fire engine house, though historically, the building stood several feet beneath this monument. A railroad embankment covers the building's original street-level location. (nypl)

Virginia's and the Federal government's upper echelons reacted swiftly to the shocking news. Henry Wise ordered more of his state's militia to react and go to Harpers Ferry. The governor himself then boarded a train bound for the scene of the action.

Secretary of War Floyd and President Buchanan likewise moved to suppress the riotous actions at Harpers Ferry. The nearest Federal Army troops to Harpers Ferry immediately at Floyd's disposal were at Fort Monroe on the tip of the Virginia peninsula. There, Capt. Edward Ord commanded 150 artillerymen. Having few other options, this seemed to be the most expeditious measure. He ordered Ord's command to depart for Harpers Ferry immediately. Floyd also appointed a commander of this force of United States Regulars: Lt. Col. Robert E. Lee. Taking pen in hand, the war secretary drafted Lee's orders.

Keeping all of this news quiet was difficult, as J. E. B. Stuart's visit to the War Department shows. The ambitious lieutenant immediately saw an opportunity. He had just come from Lee's home; he could carry the orders to him. Stuart set off searching for Lee and eventually found him in the Stabler-Leadbeater Apothecary Shop in Alexandria. Lee opened the brief note and immediately rode to the War Department. Stuart volunteered his services to Lee.

The pair of officers reached Secretary Floyd's office as quickly as their mounts carried them. There, Floyd hastily briefed Lee about the measures currently adopted, which included Ord's force and the addition of 86 Marines stationed at the Washington Navy Yard. Wasting little time, Floyd, Lee, and Stuart walked across the lawn to the Executive Mansion to confer with the President.

Floyd and the two officers found Buchanan troubled by the latest reports. Uncertainty remained about the size of this insurrectionary force. Would 150 men be enough? Could they even reach the town in time to make a difference? By the time Floyd, Lee, and Stuart arrived in his office, Buchanan was able to scrounge up two companies of Frederick militia that offered their services. The President told Lee to take command of this force, the United States Marine detachment, and any other armed forces—Regulars or militia—in Harpers Ferry and subdue this uprising.

With their orders in hand, Lee and Stuart rushed to catch the 1:00 p.m. train out of the capital in such haste that Lee did not even have the chance to return home. He scribbled a note to his family about his departure and, in civilian clothes, rode to the train station. Stuart likewise wore civilian clothes when he rode into Washington on the morning of October 17. He, however, managed to borrow a sword and military coat before departing the War Department.

Stuart's and Lee's exit from the capital was slightly delayed and they missed the train by 20 minutes. However, the agents of the Baltimore and Ohio Railroad recognized the importance of the men's mission—after all, it was their trains that could not pass through Harpers Ferry—and quickly forwarded a single locomotive and car for the two officers. In these improvised accommodations, Lee and Stuart sped off for Harpers Ferry.

The detachment of United States Marines from the Washington Navy Yard was on the tracks ahead of Stuart and Lee. Lieutenant Israel Greene commanded them. Major William W. Russell, the paymaster, accompanied the 86 Marines and two three-inch howitzers. When the Marines departed Washington, Greene remembered the men under his command were "exhilarated by the excitement of the occasion, which came after a long, dull season of confinement in the barracks." The troops "exceedingly" enjoyed their trip along the tracks of the Baltimore and Ohio Railroad to Sandy Hook, about one and a half miles east of Harpers Ferry. They reached their destination opposite beleaguered Harpers Ferry around 11 p.m. on the evening of October 17. Lee and Stuart arrived one hour later.

At Sandy Hook, Lee found not only Greene's Marines but also the companies of Frederick militia and several militia companies from Baltimore. He dictated orders for the Maryland militia to remain in Sandy Hook for the time being while he personally brought the Marines into Harpers Ferry.

*   *   *

The patter of rain mixed with the cadence of the Marines' march across the Potomac River bridge. When Lee and the Marines arrived on Virginia's soil, Harpers Ferry had "assumed quite a military appearance." Militiamen ringed the east end of the armory yard to prevent Brown's escape. No shots punctuated the wet night, but yells of the drunken revelry by various citizens and militiamen already on the scene provided a backdrop. The thick air was alive with the tension that built up over the previous day.

Inside the darkness of the engine house, John Brown and his shrinking band of followers and hostages found space to sleep on the cold brick floor. It was no plush featherbed but the exertions of the previous day undoubtedly brought quick sleep to some. Still, the noise of the drunken crowd penetrated into the room. Those who could not find sleep under the circumstances shivered through the cold, wet night.

Oliver Brown's moans and pleas for help continued throughout the night as he stretched out in one of the room's corners. "He begged again and again to be shot," recalled John Thomas Allstadt, the son. The elder Brown snarled at his son's pleading.

HARPER'S FERRY INSURRECTION—INTERIOR OF THE ENGINE-HOUSE, JUST BEFORE THE GATE IS BROKEN DOWN BY THE STORMING PARTY—COL. WASHINGTON AND HIS ASSOCIATES AS CAPTIVES, HELD BY BROWN AS HOSTAGES.

"Oh you will get over it," said Brown. "If you must die, die like a man." After a prolonged silence from that dark corner, Brown called out to his son. Oliver did not respond. "I guess he is dead," said the father.

While some of Brown's party tried to rest, the few sentinels at the doorway struggled to see much of anything outside through the pitch darkness and rain. Lee utilized this natural cover to replace the militia surrounding the engine house with the troop of Marines, thus containing Brown's force and preventing its escape. The experienced army officer was confident that he held the upper hand in the current situation. "But for the fear of sacrificing the lives of some of the gentlemen held . . . as prisoners in a midnight assault, I should have ordered the attack at once," Lee reported. Instead, he spent the early morning hours before the sun rose plotting a course of action for a dawn assault. Initially, Lee offered the militia the chance to capture or kill Brown in the upcoming assault. Colonel Edward Shriver of the Frederick contingent, who assumed overall command of the militia around Harpers Ferry, declined the honor. "These men of mine have wives and children at home. I will not expose them to such risks. You are paid for doing this kind of work." The other militia commanders agreed. The task fell to the Marines.

Lee worried about the lives of Brown's prisoners during such an assault. Accordingly, he "determined to summon the insurgents to surrender." An attack

Many people stood inside the engine house at the moment of the Marines' attack. Brown's hostages can be seen standing along the wall on the image's left while Brown and his men prepare to defend themselves. (loc)

was the last resort. While waiting for the sun to appear above the horizon, Lee drafted the directive.

Lee's summons were stern and direct. He demanded the immediate surrender of Brown and his force. "If they will peaceably surrender themselves and restore the pillaged property, they shall be kept in safety to await the orders of the President. Colonel Lee represents to them, in all frankness, that it is impossible for them to escape; that the armory is surrounded on all sides by troops; and that if he is compelled to take them by force he cannot answer for their safety." For Brown and his men, trapped in their current situation, Lee thought it might be an attractive offer.

At 6:30 a.m., the first glint of sunlight lit Harpers Ferry's dark streets and buildings. Lee conferred with Marine commander Lt. Greene and ordered him "to select a detail of twelve men for a storming party." Greene picked "twelve of my best men" and selected another twelve for a reserve. Utilizing the last hint of darkness for concealment, Greene's party maneuvered behind the engine house and deployed on its west side, adjacent to the watchman's room. A brick partition separated the room Brown occupied and the watchman's room, thus keeping Greene's storming party hidden from the raiders' view.

Lee directed that, should Brown decline the entreaty, the Marines would attack with only the bayonet in order to ensure the safety of the hostages,. In the early morning hours, before the sun fully illuminated Harpers Ferry, gun smoke would limit visibility inside the engine house. Lee did not want an

Harper's Weekly **recreated a scene for readers outside John Brown's fort that looked far more orderly than the events that transpired.** (loc)

errant shot fired in that chaotic situation to accidentally hit one of Brown's hostages.

As the Marines maneuvered into their assault positions, Israel Greene took stock of the task ahead. "The engine-house was a strong [brick] building," he recalled. Two large, "very strongly made" doors protected the raiders, who managed to drill small holes in the doors so that they could fire upon any assailants. Getting through the doors was the Marines' toughest task. Three of them wielded large sledge hammers to batter down the doors and gain entry.

By 7:00 a.m., Greene's storming party assumed their position on the west side of the watchman's room. Lee stood near the armory gate behind one of its pillars. There, he shielded himself from bullets but was close enough to monitor the action. Lee's men stood silently in their places. He gave the order to commence the operation.

Lee gave Brown and his men the chance to surrender before the Marines commenced the assault. Lee handed his written summons to the youthful Stuart. In his borrowed army coat and his now familiar hat, Stuart proceeded, under a white flag of truce, to the central doorway of the fire engine house. Lee instructed Stuart that he was not to be a negotiator. If the insurgents did not surrender, Stuart would signal the assault to begin.

Citizens and scores of militiamen watched from various points in Harpers Ferry as Stuart took his lonely steps towards the central door. He stood outside and informed Mr. Smith, Brown's alias, that he carried a message from Lt. Col. Lee. The door opened slightly, just four inches. There was enough light for Stuart to see Smith standing in the crack between the doors "with a cocked carbine in his hand." Stuart saw enough of the man to recognize his true identity, that of an old nemesis from Kansas, "Old Ossawattomie Brown." The cavalryman handed Lee's message to Brown.

In a few moments, Brown grasped the crux of Lee's terms, and he did not like them. He had terms of his own and proffered them to Stuart. Brown "presented his propositions in every possible shape with admirable tact," Stuart remembered. However, Stuart was under orders to not negotiate under any circumstances with the raiders. Regardless, Lee never would have accepted Brown's terms—that he and his men be allowed to escape. Stuart denied Brown's compromise.

A diorama at the Marine Corps Museum portrays the attack on Brown's fort. (cm)

The hostages listened to the parlay, hoping terms could be reached and their lives would not be endangered. They, too, pleaded with Stuart for Lee to see them. One dissenting voice, that of Lewis Washington, piped up. "Never mind us, Fire!" he said. Near the armory gate, Lee recognized Washington's voice and supposedly proclaimed, "The old revolutionary blood does tell!"

Negotiations came to an end. Stuart peeled away from the engine house door and waved his hat. Greene saw this predetermined signal and yelled for his men to begin their assault. Brown quickly slammed the door as the first wave of Marines rushed forward. Guns poked out of the manmade portholes in the building and Brown's remaining men fired at their assailants.

Greene ordered three Marines with sledge hammers to the front. In unison, each man pounded his large hammer into the heavy wooden doors, which were further supported by ropes on the inside. Their swings hardly made an impression in the wood. The Marine lieutenant realized the hammer blows were futile and recalled his men.

Greene next spied a heavy ladder laid out in the armory yard. Above the sporadic gunfire, he directed his assaulting party to pick up the ladder and pound down the doors with it. A moment of silence gripped the scene while the Marines changed tactics. When all was ready, the reserve stood by in support while the assaulting party, ladder in hand, lunged towards the door. They ran forward and rammed the door with their impromptu ram. The ladder slammed into the heavy door, immediately bringing the Marines' running feet to a halt. Their forceful battering made an impression but the doorway still remained closed. The storming party backed up and tried a second time. They pointed the head of the ladder at the same spot where the first blow struck the door. Greene ordered his men to run forward again. Within a moment, the ladder burst "a ragged hole low down in the right-hand door," Greene reported. The sound of splintering wood mixed with the gunfire.

By now, a heavy layer of smoke floated in the armory yard and clouded the fire engine room. But Greene, from his position between the doors of the watchman's room and the central door to the fire engine house, noticed the splintered opening. Dropping to all fours, Greene led his men into the engine room.

Lewis Washington huddled in the rear of the room, watching all of this transpire. Washington admired Brown's tenacity in this moment, calling him "the coolest and firmest man I ever saw in defying death and danger." Brown "commanded his men with

After their attempt to break the doors of the engine house with sledgehammers failed, the Marines resorted to a heavy ladder to force entry into Brown's makeshift fort. (cm)

The armory's fire engine house has forever been known as John Brown's Fort following the 1859 raid. (loc)

the utmost composure, encouraging them to be firm and to sell their lives as dearly as they could." While watching Brown's deadly work, Washington, through the smoke, saw the blue uniform of a Marine crawl through the doorway.

This was Lt. Greene. The Marines' makeshift battering ram had splintered the heavy central door to the room at just the moment Brown stopped to reload. In the chaos of the moment, Brown's defenders missed Greene's entry. The lieutenant sprang to his feet and darted to the rear of the room, where he met Washington.

Brown's men, their guns reloaded, opened fire again on the storming Marines. Major Russell, the Marine paymaster, followed behind Greene, armed only with a rattan switch cane. Both passed inside safely. Behind them, Private Luke Quinn did not. Just as he crossed the threshold of the engine house, a bullet slammed into his abdomen and soon brought his life to an end. Marine Mathew Ruppert likewise received a slight wound in the face.

Back at the room's rear, Washington extended his hand to Greene before pointing to a man "on one knee…with a carbine in his hand, just pulling the lever to reload." "This is Ossawatomie," said Washington. Above the din of the guns, Brown heard Washington's comment and turned to face Greene. Immediately, Greene lunged forward and swung his sword at Brown's head. The blow missed, instead giving Brown "a deep saber cut in the back of the neck," knocking

Brown to the floor. Lieutenant Greene swung again and this time stabbed at Brown's left breast. In the haste of the Marines' deployment to Harpers Ferry, Greene brought with him only his light sword. Greene struck Brown with such force that "the blade bent double."

As Greene neutralized Brown, the rest of his storming party trickled through the small hole in the door. A handful of Marines gained passage and immediately used their cold steel to subdue the insurgents. While the Marines were in the process of gaining entry, some of Brown's men inside panicked and attempted to surrender. "Sir, you can do as you please," Brown told one of the Marines, while others continued to fire at the storming party. Greene's orders to them were "to capture, or, if necessary, kill, the insurgents, and take possession of the engine-house." Accordingly, one Marine stabbed Dauphin Thompson with his bayonet while Thompson scurried for cover under a fire engine. Another bayoneted Jeremiah Anderson to the back wall of the room so forcefully that the raider was pinned there for some time and eventually twisted upside down.

The maelstrom inside the engine house ended almost as quickly as it began. Lee reported, "The whole was over in a few minutes." Greene more specifically remembered, "The whole fight had not lasted over three minutes." With the killing at an end, Greene paused in the engine room and noted that it "was thick with smoke, and it was with difficulty that a person could be seen across the room." The Marines quickly began to sort out prisoners from raiders. Brown's prisoners, now freed after many hours of terror, uncertainty, and panic, "were the sorriest lot of people I ever saw," wrote the Marine lieutenant.

*   *   *

While the hostages wandered freely from their jail of the last two days, Marines carried Brown out of the engine house and laid him on the grass nearby. Armed Marines stood guard around him and the other members of Brown's force who were now prisoners but found protecting them to be a difficult task. "The pent-up feelings of the spectators found appropriate expression in a general shout," noted one onlooker. An angry and interested crowd pressed against the Marine barrier to get a glimpse at the ringleader of the raid. Lee subsequently ordered a few men to carry

Brown outside the armory yard and lay him on the floor of the paymaster's office. Aaron Stevens soon joined his commander there.

Outside the paymaster's office, the euphoria of the past thirty-six hours did not fade away for the civilians and militia that participated in this historic event. Yet Brown's raid on their town and subsequent capture were still too fresh to put into perspective. Chaos and the stench of death still clung to the streets. "I saw the town crowded with military of all arms, uniforms, and in all stages of organization from the quiet effective looking United States Marines to the half armed, half drunk and noisy militiamen," noted the recently arrived David Hunter Strother.

> In the Potomac River lay three dead bodies which the armed mob were shooting at for their amusement. In the street near the old arsenal lay the bloody corpse of a negro [Dangerfield Newby] whose glassy staring eyes and fallen jaw was hideous to behold. A dog was smelling the mass of coagulated blood which surrounded his head and a couple of pigs were rooting at the body. In the engine house and armory yard lay three other bodies ghastly and stiff while beside the wall lay another man, said to be Jerry [Jeremiah] Anderson, wallowing in death spasms and half clothed in vestiments [sic] grimed with dirt and blood.

Even before the blood was washed off the streets and as the gun smoke still hung low in the armory yard, Robert E. Lee began gathering evidence about Brown and his men while the crime scene remained authentic. Lee tallied the town's losses. Four civilians died during the raid and one Marine, Luke Quinn, perished from his wounds received in the engine house. Brown's men wounded nine others—one civilian, one Marine, and seven militiamen. Additionally, one slave, Jim, who joined Brown's command, drowned in the action near the Shenandoah River.

A few hours after capturing Brown, Lee followed up on leads in Maryland. He dispatched the Baltimore Independent Grays to return to their home state and find John Cook. Additionally, Lee tasked them with locating Brown's weapons cache across the river. The Baltimore militia "found the boxes of arms (Sharp's carbines and belt revolvers), and recovered Mr. Washington's wagon and horses," Lee reported.

Lee had another job for the Marines. While Lieutenant Greene and a handful of men stood guard over the prisoners, Lee ordered Stuart and a small force to find "Old Brown's house," the Kennedy farm, "and see what there was there." Stuart walked alongside the men temporarily under his command the 4.5 miles to Brown's hideout. Looters and souvenir seekers already had visited the site by the time Stuart's force arrived and were quickly shuffled out, leaving behind most of the evidence.

Inside the farmhouse, Stuart found "the magazine of pikes, blankets[,] clothing of every kind, and utensils of every sort." Better yet, Brown left all of his correspondence and that of his men as well as his plans unburned. Within hours of his capture, Brown's enemies knew everything they could have hoped for from Stuart's discovery: the size of his force, his plan and expectations, and his goal. After sifting through the documents, Lee concluded, "The result proves that the plan was the attempt of a fanatic or madman, which could end only in failure; and its temporary success was owing to the panic and confusion he succeeded in creating by magnifying his numbers." Clearly, Brown's strategy failed to impress Lee's three-plus decades of military service.

Meanwhile, Brown and Stevens lay on the floor of the paymaster's office, struggling from their wounds. Stevens, described Strother, lay "in the last stages of exhaustion." Brown's wounds were fresher. "The old man's strongly marked face, iron grey hair and white beard were grimed and matted with blood and fresh puddles oozing from wounds in his head collected on the floor and traveling bag."

At 1 p.m., Virginia's governor Henry Wise reached Harpers Ferry via train from Richmond.

Newspaper correspondents and politicians interrogated Brown shortly after his capture. Soon, Brown began to weaponize his voice in the cause of freedom. (flin)

Having missed the action, he immediately wanted to interview the prisoners, especially Brown. A sizable group of dignitaries had also reached the town, including Senator James Mason of Virginia, Congressmen Clement Vallandigham of Ohio and Charles Faulkner of Virginia, and attorney Andrew Hunter. Together, they visited Brown.

Before any of the visitors questioned the wounded man, Lee told Brown that, if he so desired, he would bar any further visits to the paymaster's office. Brown said to the lieutenant colonel that he was "glad to make himself and his motives clearly understood." Thus began a three hour interview, called by one Brown biographer a "dramatic" scene "upon which the shadows of coming events were more ominously cast" than almost any other in the antebellum period.

Brown, to his credit and despite his wounds, answered the barrage of questions. He spoke confidently and claimed to have acted alone. The prisoner did not want his captors to think of him as a murderer or madman. "I had thirty-odd prisoners, whose wives and daughters were in tears for their safety, and I felt for them," he admitted. "I wanted to allay the fears of those who believed we came here to burn and kill." Brown evoked the Golden Rule—"Do unto others as you would that others should do unto you"—as his justification for staging this raid "to free the slaves, and only that."

Despite his feelings, Brown supposedly felt for the families of his prisoners, and in his otherwise "cool, collected and indomitable" manner in Wise's words, he did not mince words with his interviewers. To a newspaper reporter who would soon print Brown's words for everyone across the United States to read, Brown warned Southern slaveholders. "I wish to say, furthermore, that you had better—

Harpers Ferry's citizens moved quickly to bury the remains of the dead insurgents. (loc)

all you people at the South—prepare yourselves for a settlement of that question that must come up for settlement sooner than you are prepared for it," he began. "The sooner you are prepared the better. You may dispose of me very easily; I am nearly disposed of now; but this question is still to be settled—this negro question I mean—the end of that is not yet." This was not the last time Brown warned of future bloodshed to settle that question. And whether it was his words or his actions that spurred them to make necessary changes to protect their way of life, Virginians and southerners as a whole heeded what Brown said. The sooner they prepared, the better.

The cessation of hostilities on Tuesday, October 18, did not restore the pre-raid bucolic atmosphere in Harpers Ferry. "Night soon came," wrote Joseph Rosengarten of the Pennsylvania Railroad, "and it was made hideous by the drunken noise and turmoil of the crowd in the village." Inside the Wager House Hotel, Wise and his staff reviewed the contraband material captured from Brown's hideout at the Kennedy Farm.

On Wednesday morning, magistrates of Jefferson County, Virginia, and the United States orchestrated the removal of Brown and his prisoners to the county seat, Charlestown. Of Brown's force of twenty-two men, including Brown, ten died during the raid. Brown and seven others were ultimately captured. Yet not all of Brown's men met death for their roles in the raid.

The group of five men who fled the Kennedy farm on October 17—John Cook, Charles Tidd, Owen Brown, Barclay Coppoc, and Francis Meriam—hid during daylight hours and traveled at night during their trek north towards the Pennsylvania line. Cook was the first of the party captured after being identified near Mont Alto, Pennsylvania, on October 26. Two days later he arrived at the Jefferson County Jail in Charlestown. Brown, Coppoc, Meriam, and Tidd all continued onto Chambersburg, where Meriam caught a train to Philadelphia. The others continued cross-country to Centre County, Pennsylvania, before separating on November 24. Brown headed back to Ohio, Coppoc back to Springdale, Iowa, and Tidd to the safety of Chatham. All four men lived—even if only for a short time—to tell of their role in John Brown's war against slavery.

Albert Hazlett and Osborne Anderson made their escape from the arsenal on the night of October 17. They crossed the Potomac on a small boat before taking to the woods. The pair returned to the Kennedy farmhouse and the schoolhouse but found both places deserted. Heading due north, they reached the Pennsylvania border within four days, though Hazlett was incapacitated with blisters on his feet. He implored Anderson to continue on without him. "I was loth [sic] to leave him," recalled Anderson, "as we both knew that danger was more imminent [in Pennsylvania] than when in the mountains around Harper's [sic]

Ferry." Hazlett was captured on October 22 near Newville, Pennsylvania, while Anderson caught a train to Philadelphia and eventually to Chatham. Hazlett sat behind bars in Carlisle before being extradited back to Charlestown on November 5.

During Lt. Greene's removal of the prisoners on October 19 from Harpers Ferry to a waiting train on the tracks of the Winchester and Potomac Railroad, shouts from angry bystanders rang out, "Lynch them! Lynch them!" Wise quickly ended such vents of anger. "Oh, it would be cowardly to do so now!" The crowd subsided. It soon dispersed from Harpers Ferry altogether as the train carrying John Brown, Aaron Stevens, Shields Green, and Barclay Coppoc chugged towards Charlestown. There, Brown and the other captives would have their fates decided not by an angry rabble or Marines at Harpers Ferry but instead by a jury of their peers.

The monument marking the original location of John Brown's Fort is accessible via stairs or a walking path. Another nearby stairwell leads visitors down the railroad embankment and into the armory archaeological site. (cm)

"The Crimes of This Guilty Land"

John Brown's Imprisonment, Trial, and Execution

CHAPTER SEVEN

OCTOBER 19, 1859 -
DECEMBER 2, 1859

Jefferson County's seat, Charlestown, provided the backdrop to the last act of John Brown's life. His raid at an end, Brown still had a role to play in the burning question of slavery in America. This time, though, rather than a broadsword or Sharps carbine, he played it with a pen from behind the iron doors of his jail cell, and from the courtroom at Charlestown.

Aside from Harpers Ferry's and Bolivar's citizens, the people of Charlestown were the first to hear the shocking news of Brown's attack and some of the first to respond in an organized fashion (at least, as organized as Virginia's militia system could be). Unfortunately for the town's citizens, the excitement of Brown's raid rippled throughout their lives for several more months. "The noise and confusion, the hustle and bustle consequent upon the collection of so large a body of troops in a country village continue unabated," an eyewitness recorded.

Like many other Southern towns, the heart of Charlestown was in its town square. The county courthouse stood on the northeast corner of the town square. Over a six-week period, this courthouse provided the setting for the last phase of John Brown's

Jefferson County's Courthouse served as the backdrop for the final, and arguably most important, chapter of John Brown's life.
(kp)

public life. Jailer John Avis confined Brown and the other captured raiders catty-corner to the courthouse. The jail building held the appearance of a house—Avis and his family did live in its front portion—but its enclosed backyard and barred windows betrayed its otherwise innocent appearance. Brown bided his time here while Virginia and the Federal government decided his fate.

Virginia's authorities clamored for a speedy trial and a quick end to the John Brown story. It just so happened that the regional Circuit Court had recently begun its session in Charlestown. If the trial were not held soon, then it would not be possible to start it until April 1860. Constant fear and rumors of abolitionist plots to free Brown and his imprisoned associates would have meant a long term of service for the state's militia. Additionally, during that stretch of time, the entire state would be on edge, wondering if Brown's arraignment might happen. Thus, Virginia was granted relief by the Circuit Court's presence in Charlestown.

Soon, another question arose. Brown and his raiders had occupied a Federal armory and arsenal complex. His crimes were against the United States government as well as Virginia's. However, Governor Henry Wise insisted that Virginia would have jurisdiction over the trials. Brown biographer Oswald Villard articulated Wise's reasons for not involving the Federal government: "the nearest Federal prison was at some distance [from Harpers Ferry], and Wise had no desire to have it said that the State of Virginia was forced to hide behind the skirts of the Federal Government, and to obtain its help to punish those who violated her soil and killed her citizens." For most of the raid, Virginians had fought Brown's men. Now, they would finish the battle they began.

Virginia and Henry Wise soon discovered that John Brown would not fold over in this fight. And worse yet, Brown's words and actions in the last month and a half of his life elevated him to a stature he never would have reached had Israel Greene's sword finished the job and killed him.

At 10:30 a.m. on October 25, one week after Marines removed Brown from the engine house, the heavy iron door to John Brown's cell swung open. John Avis latched Brown and Edwin Coppoc together. Aaron Stevens, Shields Green, and John Copeland trailed their leader. Brown "seemed weak and his eyes were swollen from wounds on his head" as he stepped out of the jail into Charlestown's main intersection. Armed men stood diagonally across the juncture from the jail door to the courthouse door. When Brown's party reached that house of justice, they found another guard stationed there. "The court house was bristling with bayonets on all sides," wrote an eyewitness. Cannon aimed directly at Brown's cell.

Governor Wise took stringent military measures to ensure no scheming abolitionists freed Brown, which was a constant fear. These security measures meant that the number of casual observers to Brown's trial remained small.

But these security measures required large contingents of militia. Moreover, there were large numbers of attending newspaper correspondents. The press could not get enough coverage of this story. In the week since the raid, newspapers across the North and South editorialized Brown's actions—southern papers described Brown as a madman or murderer, while "not one [Northern newspaper] wholeheartedly supported Brown," said Brown biographer David S. Reynolds. The newspapers extended the telegraph lines from Harpers Ferry to Charlestown to accommodate speedy coverage of the trial. Brown's platform was a large one, as northerners and southerners daily followed the news brought by the telegraph.

Judge Richard Parker accepted the prisoners into the courtroom. The examining court, which determined if there was enough cause for a trial, consisted of eight slaveholders. Andrew Hunter, Wise's hand selected pick to prosecute Brown and the others, stood at a table as the prisoners entered (Hunter determined to speedily prosecute Brown, promising to have him "arraigned, tried, found guilty, sentenced, and hung, all within ten days"). Once the throng settled into the room and quieted down, the proceedings commenced.

The court presented the five prisoners with the charges being pressed against them: first-degree murder, treason against the Old Dominion, and conspiring to foment a slave insurrection. Judge Parker asked how the defendants pled. Given his opening on a national stage, Brown slowly rose to address not just those in the courthouse but all Virginians and Americans. Wise promised a fair trial to him, Brown began, but, "under no circumstances whatever, will I be able to have a fair trial. If you seek my blood, you can have it any moment, without this mockery

Andrew Hunter was the prosecuting attorney against John Brown. He was a loyal Confederate during the Civil War. His cousin, Maj. Gen. David Hunter, burned Andrew's home outside Charlestown in July 1864. (loc)

of a trial. I have had no counsel. I have not been able to advise with any one." Despite his wounds, Brown continued:

> *If we are forced with a mere form—a trial for execution—you might spare yourselves that trouble. I am ready for my fate. I do not ask for a trial. I beg no mockery of a trial—no insult—nothing but that which conscience gives, or cowardice would drive you to practise [sic]. I ask again to be excused from this mockery of a trial. I do not know what is to be the benefit of it to the Commonwealth. I have now little further to ask, other than that I may not be foolishly insulted, only as cowardly barbarians insult those who fall into their power.*

Clearly, Brown was not going down easy.

The magistrate court assigned Lawson Botts and Charlestown's mayor Thomas C. Green to Brown's legal team. These men were the first in a long list of attorneys to represent Brown. On Brown's behalf, they pleaded "not guilty" to the three charges leveled against Brown and the four others. The prisoners asked for separate trials, a request the court granted.

John Brown was a fighter. Whether he was in Kansas, Harpers Ferry, or the courtroom, he fought. His trial was no different than any other stage of his life. Brown crafted a legally dubious defense for his attorneys. He claimed "that he had not come to Harper's [sic] Ferry with malicious intent," says historian Brian McGinty in his book on the trial,

Brown, recovering from his wounds suffered during the raid, can be seen on the cot in the center of the packed Jefferson County Courthouse in the midst of his trial. (w)

that he intended no injury against Harpers Ferry's citizens but only wanted to aid the local slaves in their desire to "win their freedom." Of course, the death of four civilians and the innumerable shots fired would make that tough to prove in the courtroom. Brown's insistence on this strategy meant that Botts and Green did not have much to argue with. Brown's legal team focused on presenting their client's benevolent treatment of his prisoners as the crux of their defense.

Judge Parker pounded his gavel and commenced Brown's trial on Thursday morning, October 27. That day, though he was still reclining on his cot, Brown "looked considerably better, the swelling having left his eyes."

Immediately, Lawson Botts opened by reading a dispatch he'd received the previous day from A. H. Lewis of Akron, Ohio. Lewis claimed to be familiar with members of Brown's family. "Insanity is hereditary in that family," he wrote. When Botts and Green showed Brown the telegram in his jail cell on October 26, Brown admitted parts of it were true but "of other portions he is ignorant." Brown, caught unawares by Botts's apparent life-saving move, rejected the tactic. His legal team sought another delay in the trial to allow Brown's team to properly consult with their client. Judge Parker denied this request and also threw out the insanity plea, since "it was not presented in a reliable form."

For the next few days, the defense and prosecution teams questioned multiple witnesses to the events in Harpers Ferry. This list included Dr. Starry, Conductor Phelps, Lewis Washington, Archibald Kitzmiller, and others. Henry Hunter, Andrew's son, spoke of his part in the killing of William Thompson.

In the Friday afternoon session, with the gallows looming ever closer, Brown once again appealed to the court, claiming that his trial was unfair and that the witnesses he called to testify had not appeared. Additionally, Brown did not trust his defense team to save him from conviction, though they performed as well as they could have under the circumstances. He asked for a delay. Judge Parker denied the request.

Near the trial's end, Brown's defense team did receive a shake-up. Young lawyer George Hoyt of Massachusetts arrived in Charlestown under the guise of helping Brown in the courtroom. In reality, Hoyt's mission was to gather information for a planned jailbreak to free Brown, and to destroy some of Brown's letters that might be used to incriminate prominent northerners in the Harpers Ferry scheme.

The news of Brown's Raid had sent the Secret Six into a panic. After all, these men had spent years financing Brown's operations and were privy to his most intimate plans. Their fears of prosecution for complicity in Brown's plan were reasonable. Franklin Sanborn quickly departed for Canada, as did Brown's confidant Frederick Douglass. Gerrit Smith was committed to an insane asylum. Theodore Parker was safe in Rome and would soon be safe in the grave, dying of tuberculosis in 1860. Samuel Gridley Howe remained in Boston, as did Thomas Wentworth Higginson. Once boasting that he was always ready to invest in treason, Higginson remained defiant and unapologetic.

Before the trial's conclusion, Botts and Green withdrew and Washington attorney Samuel Chilton and Clevelander Hiram Griswold took their place along Brown's side. Regardless of the defense team's composition, Judge Parker's and Andrew Hunter's insistence on a quick trial—supported by Wise's similar feelings—ultimately won over. On October 31, both sides presented their closing arguments. Brown's team clung to the assertion that their client could not be guilty of treason to Virginia because he was not a citizen of the state and thus owed it nothing. Brown's raid, they continued, did not begin a slave rebellion nor was it ever likely to have done so.

Once Griswold returned to his seat, Hunter stood before the packed courtroom. Brown's malice was calculated, he claimed, and it was all part of a premeditated plan "to take possession of the Commonwealth and make it another Haiti," a reference to the slave revolt there over fifty years earlier. Hunter's conjuring of a deadly but successful slave rebellion sent the jury on its way to deliberate.

Shields Green (left), John Copeland (center), and Albert Hazlett (right) await trial from their Charlestown jail cell. (loc)

John Cook and Edwin Coppoc were two of the four raiders executed in Charlestown on December 16, 1859, as depicted here. (loc)

Forty-five minutes later, they returned. Crowds filled every corner of the courtroom and even stood outside to hear the jury's decision. They concluded in the affirmative that Brown was guilty of all three counts charged against him. Upon hearing this, the stoic Brown lay down on his cot "as if he had no interest in the proceedings."

Judge Parker gave Brown two days to ruminate on his guilt. On November 2, while the jury pondered the evidence in Edwin Coppoc's case, Brown arrived in the courtroom again to hear his sentence. Did he have any reason why he should not be charged, asked the court. Brown, who reclined on his cot for most of the trial and appeared indifferent to most of the proceedings, slowly rose to his feet and stood fully erect. "I have, may it please the Court, a few words to say," he began. "[W]ith perfect calmness of voice and mildness of manner," Brown continued his spontaneous statement.

First, Brown denied that he planned on his raid leading to violence. If this attack had been waged to aid "the so-called great" or any of their acquaintances rather than the enslaved, "this Court would have deemed it an act worthy of reward rather than punishment," he claimed. Next, Brown invoked God and the Bible to justify his acts:

> *This Court acknowledges, too, as I suppose, the validity of the law of God. I see a book kissed, which I suppose to be the Bible, or at least the New Testament, which teaches me that all things whatsoever I would that men should do to me, I should do even so to them.*

It teaches me, further, to remember them that are in bonds as bound with them. I endeavored to act up to that instruction.

Still standing upright, Brown confirmed his belief that, acting under God's law and "in behalf of His despised poor, I did no wrong, but right." Furthermore, he continued, "if it is deemed necessary that I should forfeit my life for the furtherance of the ends of justice, and mingle my blood further with the blood of my children and with the blood of millions in this slave country whose rights are disregarded by wicked, cruel, and unjust enactments, I say, let it be done."

After Brown concluded his address to the court, Judge Parker sentenced Brown to be executed by public hanging on December 2, one month away. The sentenced man received his death warrant silently. While the rest of the courtroom's occupants reflected his quiet demeanor, one man clapped upon hearing Parker's decision. The crowd quickly suppressed this act and quietly stood by as Brown left the room en route to his familiar jail cell.

As quick as Brown exited the courtroom, his words raced through telegraph wires across the country. Northerners and southerners alike read them in their local newspapers. Both had very different reactions.

In the North, Brown's words galvanized supporters to his cause. He appealed to God, a "higher law," as William Seward called it in his own fight against pro-slavery supporters. Ralph Waldo Emerson later coupled Brown's dialogue with Abraham Lincoln's Gettysburg Address as the two greatest pieces of oratory in American history.

Southerners, who were admirably impressed by Brown's stoicism and bravery, now charted a different course. In Brown's peaceful words and his previous violent actions, they conjured ties between Brown's crusade and that of the Republican Party. Fire-Eater Edmund Ruffin procured a handful of Brown's pikes and gave one to each slave state Governor to ornament their state's legislative chambers. Attached to each pike, Ruffin scrawled a message: "To the State of _____. Sample of the Favors Designed for Us by Our Northern Brethren." Let the Republicans gain power, Ruffin and other powerful southerners insinuated, and pikes like these would stab the heart of Southern society.

Judge Parker's selection of December 2 as the date of Brown's execution gave concerned parties a chance to voice their opinions about Brown. In an attempt to spare him from the gallows, Brown's legal team, influenced by Montgomery Blair, tried to label Brown as insane, a diagnosis perpetuated by some historians even today. However, Brown biographer Stephen Oates disregards the gathered affidavits as biased evidence (after all, they were collected to save Brown's life). Furthermore, says Oates, "to label him a 'maniac' out of touch with 'reality' is to ignore the piercing insight he had into what his raid—whether it succeeded or whether it failed—would do to sectional tensions that already existed between North and South." Numerous concerned parties bombarded Governor Wise with similar pleas to let Brown live but all to no avail. The insanity claims were disregarded and the execution date held firm.

Other friends of Brown worked feverishly to pull together a last-minute scheme to free him from his cell. Brown buried any attempts to do so. He now faced the gallows and saw his fate in front of him. "I am worth inconceivably more to hang than for any other purpose," he claimed. Regardless, Southern fears of such a plot persisted until the date Brown was hanged. Virginia militia flooded Charlestown to ensure order and the execution of Brown and his raiders.

Edmund Ruffin used Brown's pikes to propagate the idea of future Northern aggression against the South. (npg)

Charlestown's streets and Governor Wise's office were not the only Virginia settings inundated with visitors and letters. Brown received and answered letters from his cell and spoke with hundreds of visitors, including the press corps that continued to portray a brave man ready to meet his fate. Haters and admirers wrote to Brown and saw him chained in the Charlestown jail. Citizens on both sides of the widening abyss in the United States—an abyss that Brown's raid and prosecution did much to widen—continued to strengthen their feelings about Brown, both positive and negative.

One letter Brown received was from Mahala Doyle, widow of John Doyle, three years removed from the massacre at Pottawatomie Creek. Doyle wrote to Brown in his Charlestown jail cell, recalling the events of that night along the Pottawatomie. She did not believe Brown had murdered her husband and sons to free the slaves. "We had none and never expected to own one," she insisted. Instead, Brown's actions only made her "a poor disconsolate widow with helpless children." She closed her letter with a reference to her youngest son, whom Brown had spared that night. He was now grown, and "is very desirous to be at Charlestown on the day of your execution . . . he might adjust the rope around your neck if Gov. Wise would permit it."

Also writing letters was Annie Brown, "watch dog" of her father's army at the Kennedy farmhouse. On November 29, Annie wrote to a friend, begging for an intercession to Governor Wise to have her father's body returned to his family following the execution. "We see a great many attribute father's course to a spirit of revenge, but it is utterly false," Annie believed. "He was actuated by a noble, generous feeling which has been growing in his breast for more than 20 years." Ever defiant, Annie frankly testified that "if our dear father (as well as brothers) are to be sacrificed to the God of Slavery, we shall not believe they had died in vain."

On December 1, Brown had one last visitor, his wife Mary. Both wept upon seeing each other but shortly regained their composure. They dined with John Avis and his family, who had taken a liking to Brown, before privately talking over Brown's will, Mary's future, and schooling for their eight children. Brown lost his temper only when Mary departed—the governor specified she must remain in Harpers Ferry that night—but soon recovered himself. Brown bade his partner goodbye and returned to his cell.

Brown awoke early the next day. He turned to his Bible for strength and wisdom before turning his attention to a few last-minute earthly tasks.

One hour before the appointed time of execution, Avis opened Brown's cell door. The resolved captain gifted his Bible to his guard and his watch to jailer Avis. Brown stepped into the corridor leading from his cell to the jail's exit. On his way, he passed some of the men who pledged their life to Brown's cause: John Copeland, Shields Green, John Cook, Edwin Coppoc (all hanged on December 16, 1860), Aaron Stevens, and Albert Hazlett, the last of whom all of the captured raiders ignored in an attempt to portray the 22-year-old as not one of their own in the hopes that his life might be spared. It did not work. The state of Virginia executed Stevens and Hazlett on March 16, 1860. "God bless you, my men," Brown said to them. "May we all meet in Heaven."

Brown stepped out of the jail and witnessed the martial scene of soldiers arrayed in front of him. "I had

The jailer, John Avis, and his family lived in the front part of the jail building. Despite their different views, Avis and Brown developed a unique trust and fondness for one another. (wvsa)

no idea that Governor Wise considered my execution so important," he remarked. Indeed, Wise took many precautions to ensure no escape on the part of Brown and his men. His fears were not unwarranted. Many rumors of armed abolitionists fighting their way into Charlestown persisted. Several fires around the county seat fanned fears of slave unrest and uprising. Wise did not take any chances.

The vigilant Brown looked down from the militia lining the streets of Charlestown to see the vehicle readied to drive him to his death—a freight wagon owned by undertaker George Sadler. In the back of the wagon, Brown rode atop his coffin to the gallows recently erected in an open field south of town. He reached there about 11 a.m.

Around the gallows stood Thomas Jonathan Jackson and his Virginia Military Institute cadets, John Wilkes Booth, Edmund Ruffin, Robert E. Lee, and 1,500 other Commonwealth militia who had arrived from all corners of the state. Most of the men witnessing Brown's final act were soon destined to be caught up in the conflict Brown predicted on the day of his death. While exiting the jail, Brown handed a prophetic note to a bystander: "I John Brown am now quite certain that the crimes of this guilty land: will never be purged away; but with Blood. I had as I now think: vainly flattered myself that without very much bloodshed; it might be done." Brown's blood would be among the first to be shed.

Brown's composure, exhibited throughout the final month and a half of his life, remained intact as he ascended the gallows' steps. Militiaman Parke Poindexter, destined to die in the looming Civil War, stood near enough to take stock of Brown. He "mounted the scaffold as calmly and quietly

Brown exited the Charlestown jail and walked to sit atop his coffin on the way to the gallows amid a throng of Virginia militia. (npg)

Wheeling's Virginia Fencibles traveled the furthest distance of all Virginia's militia to be present at John Brown's execution. Here, the Fencible's orderly sergeant, George C. Trimble, sports his gaudy uniform characteristic of many prewar militia companies. (lcf)

Brown sat atop his coffin in the back of a wagon on his way to the gallows as armed militiamen guarded Charlestown. (nypl)

Brown's kissing of a slave child on his way to the gallows has become legendary, though in reality, it did not happen. Nonetheless, the story spread throughout the United States and has been popularized in many works of art. (nypl)

John Brown took his last steps ascending the gallows steps in front of hundreds of armed militiamen. (loc)

> *Charlestown, Va, 2nd December, 1859.*
> *I John Brown am now quite certain that the crimes of this guilty, land: will never be purged away; but with Blood: I had as I now think: vainly flattered myself that without very much bloodshed; it might be done.*

JOHN BROWN'S LAST PROPHECY

as if he had been going to his dinner: he did not exhibit the slightest nervous excitement or fear; not a muscle moved, nor was there the slightest nervous excitement; he stood erect and calm as if he were upon post." Brown shook hands with those near him on the scaffold and assumed his position. Avis fixed the hood and noose to Brown's head and neck. Hooded, Brown stood for ten minutes while the militia filed into their places.

Finally, all was ready. County sheriff James Campbell swung a hatchet at the rope, the trap door sprung, and Brown dangled into death. Silence shrouded the open field, pierced only by Col. John T. L. Preston's remark, "So perish all such enemies of Virginia! All such enemies of the Union! All such foes of the human race!"

Brown's limp body hung for over thirty-five minutes before it was lifted back onto the scaffolding. Fifteen doctors looked for signs of life. No pulse. John Brown was no more.

John Brown's handwritten and poignant prophecy that he handed to a bystander before departing for the gallows reads: "I John Brown am now quite certain that the crimes of this guilty land: will never be purged away; but with Blood. I had as I now think: vainly flattered myself that without very much bloodshed; it might be done." (wvsa)

"The Meteor of the War"

CONCLUSION

Members of the 13th Massachusetts Infantry removed the bell from John Brown's Fort in May 1861. Too heavy to carry with them, they entrusted it to a local citizen who kept it in her backyard. In 1892, several veterans of the regiment returned to Williamsport, Maryland, and found the bell still in the possession of Elizabeth Snyder. They raised enough money to bring the bell to their home in Marlborough, Massachusetts, where it can still be found today. (kp)

Governor Wise's precautions ensured only the Virginia militia witnessed Brown's death. But millions of people observed the timing and felt his demise. In Mary Brown's room at the Wager House Hotel, a companion looked at his watch. It was 11:15 a.m. "It is all over!" he said.

Scores of northerners marked the hour of Brown's execution in solemn tribute and remembrance. Cities, some draped in mourning, closed their shops. Orators spoke of Brown and his purpose. Bells tolled at the time of Brown's hanging.

Reports of Brown's stoicism on the day of his death enhanced his legacy in the eyes of northern abolitionists and other sympathizers. Ralph Waldo Emerson and Henry David Thoreau compared Brown's death on the gallows to Christ's sacrifice on the Cross. Mary Brown's trip through the North with her husband's remains brought crowds of adorers and those interested in getting one last look at Brown's earthly remains to the side of Brown's coffin. Relic hunters turned opportunists; pieces of the rope and scaffold that hanged Brown turned into relics of Brown's martyrdom.

On December 8, Brown's family and friends gathered outside his North Elba farm for Brown's funeral. The words of "Blow Ye the Trumpet, Blow," Brown's favored hymn, echoed across the farmstead in the Adirondack Mountains. Following a short service, pallbearers slowly lowered Brown's remains into his grave. Brown's body was no more, but his soul went marching on.

The five moves of John Brown's Fort makes it one of the most traveled buildings in the United States. (kp)

Southerners quickly noted the masses of northerners who extolled Brown's willingness to surrender his life for that of the enslaved. "[T]he Harpers Ferry invasion has advanced the cause of disunion more than any other event," said the Richmond Enquirer. "I have always been a fervid Union man," one North Carolina citizen wrote, "but I confess the endorsement of the Harper's [sic] Ferry outrage . . . has shaken my fidelity and . . . I am willing to take the chances of every possible evil that may arise from disunion, sooner than submit any longer to Northern insolence." Some Northerners tried to assuage the South's growing hostility by organizing rallies against Brown's actions. However, such demonstrations mostly fell on deaf ears.

Across the South, bands of men joined military companies. Some of these companies had fallen dormant in recent years but became alive again with renewed vigor to protect Southern institutions. "I want to knock down a John Browner so bad I dunno what to do," wrote one enthusiastic North Carolina militiaman. Virginians, situated in the Upper South near the edge of the slave owning states, armed for when the abolitionists returned. "It ought to be borne in mind that the military demonstrations at Charlestown were not intended solely to prevent a rescue, but to prepare and accustom the volunteers of Virginia for defensive operations against a more formidable foe than JOHN BROWN," the *Daily Dispatch* declared. In Shepherdstown, up the Potomac River from Harpers Ferry, the Shepherdstown Troop received a shipment of revolvers and Sharps Rifles from Governor Wise. It was his intention, the local newspaper reported, "to arm the troops along the line of the Potomac with the best of arms that can be procured."

Despite Brown's body resting peacefully in its grave in North Elba, a loud furor grew throughout the country that threatened to tear it in two. On the same day Brown's body was placed into the earth, Senator Jefferson Davis of Mississippi spoke to his colleagues in the United States Senate. "John Brown, and a thousand John Browns, can invade us, and the Government will not protect us," he declared. If the

Federal government did not protect its slaveholding states, then those states would be "released from our allegiance, and will protect ourselves out of the Union," said Davis. "To secure our rights and protect our honor we will dissever the ties that bind us together, even if it rushes us into a sea of blood."

Southerners laid the blame for Brown's raid squarely on the Republican Party. Much of their vitriol centered on William H. Seward and his prediction of an "irrepressible conflict." Seward immediately condemned Brown's actions and fought to disassociate any link between his words, his party, and Brown. But no Republican did this better than Abraham Lincoln.

On February 27, 1860, at New York City's Cooper Union, Lincoln artfully slithered between "Seward's negative fatalism and John Brown's dangerous radicalism," wrote Lincoln scholar Harold Holzer. Lincoln called Brown's plan "peculiar" and admitted "it was so absurd that the slaves, with all their ignorance, saw plainly enough it could not succeed." To further assuage Southern terror, Lincoln distanced the Republicans from Brown. "You charge that we stir insurrections among your slaves. We deny it; and what is your proof? Harper's Ferry! John Brown!! John Brown was no Republican; and you have failed to implicate a single Republican in his Harper's Ferry enterprise." Lincoln's speech propelled him to the Republican nomination for President in the 1860 Election.

Historian David Reynolds notes the connection between Brown and Lincoln's eventual victory in November 1860. "It was only through a mighty push by fire-eaters that the South could be persuaded to secede in 1860," Reynolds argues. "And their argument about the wicked aggressiveness of Northern Abolitionists would have carried little weight if John Brown had not attacked Harpers Ferry. Not only was the Republicans' choice of Lincoln largely the product of Harpers Ferry, but also the secessionists manipulated the post-Harpers Ferry frenzy to break apart the Democratic Party, dividing Lincoln's opponents." This paved the path to Lincoln's election as President, Southern secession, the American Civil War, and the end of slavery in the United States.

The Niagara Movement, a precursor to the NAACP, held a meeting at Harpers Ferry from August 15-19, 1906. Part of the meeting was a day dedicated to John Brown. They walked to John Brown's Fort on the Murphy farm and removed their shoes and socks before entering. The fort was hallowed ground. (kp)

Brown initially rested under the tombstone of his grandfather, Capt. John Brown, who died in the American Revolution. The grandson helped erect a monument over his grandfather's grave and brought this stone with him to North Elba. (nypl)

Frederick Douglass recognized John Brown's contribution to the abolition of slavery through—ironically—a failed attempt to free slaves. "When John Brown stretched forth his arm the sky was cleared. The time for compromises was gone, the armed hosts of freedom stood face to face over the chasm of a broken Union, and the clash of arms was at hand."

John Brown's 59 years of life led him to what he achieved in death. Like a meteor, he appeared quickly, caught the attention of many, and flamed out. But all those who experienced Brown's raid, who read about his trial in the newspapers, and who heard bells toll during his death hour never forgot John Brown.

> *Hanging from the beam,*
> * Slowly swaying (such the law),*
> *Gaunt the shadow on your green,*
> * Shenandoah!*
> *The cut is on the crown*
> *(Lo, John Brown),*
> *And the stabs shall heal no more.*
> *Hidden in the cap*
> * Is the anguish none can draw;*
> *So your future veils its face,*
> * Shenandoah!*
> *But the streaming beard is shown*
> *(Weird John Brown),*
> *The meteor of the war.*

Herman Melville, *The Portent*

John Brown is buried in North Elba, New York, alongside twelve of his men: Watson Brown, Oliver Brown, William Thompson, Dauphin Thompson, John Kagi, William Leeman, Jeremiah Anderson, Steward Taylor, Dangerfield Newby, Lewis Leary, Aaron Stevens, and Albert Hazlett. (nysa)

With its cobblestone streets and restored buildings, Shenandoah Street captures the historical feel of Harpers Ferry. Museums line the street, as does the park bookstore and public restrooms. (kp)

Walking Tour of Paid Sites in Lower Town Harpers Ferry

APPENDIX A

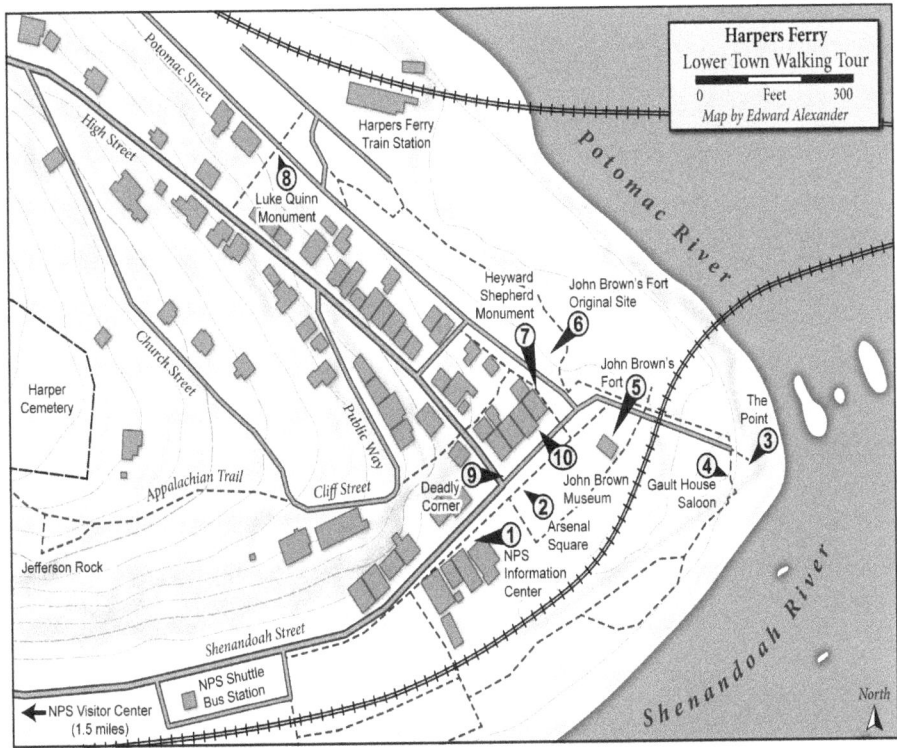

Harpers Ferry
Lower Town Walking Tour

0   Feet   300
Map by Edward Alexander

Potomac Street

High Street

Harpers Ferry
Train Station

Potomac River

8
Luke Quinn
Monument

Heyward
Shepherd
Monument

John Brown's Fort
Original Site

7   6

Church Street

Harper
Cemetery

John Brown's
Fort 5

The
Point

3

Public Way

Appalachian Trail

Cliff Street

Deadly
Corner

9

10

John Brown
Museum

2

Gault House
Saloon

4

Arsenal
Square

1

NPS
Information
Center

Jefferson Rock

Shenandoah Street

NPS Shuttle
Bus Station

NPS Visitor Center
(1.5 miles)

Shenandoah River

North

LOWER TOWN WALKING TOUR—The lower town of Harpers Ferry retains much of its "feel" from 1859 and from the Civil War years, but it is still an active town today. Be careful as you follow this walking tour. (ea)

The ripples of John Brown's October 1859 Raid traveled far beyond Jefferson County. But no place felt the immediate impact of the raid more than Harpers Ferry. This walking tour explores the Lower Town section of Harpers Ferry National Historical Park, where the major events of the raid unfolded between October 16-18, 1859.

Note: Parking in the Lower Town is extremely limited. The best parking option in this section of the park is the Harpers Ferry Train Station in one of the National Park Service designated spots on Potomac Street. If parking here is not available, it is suggested to park at the Harpers Ferry National Historical Park Visitor Center and travel to the Lower Town via the park's shuttle bus service. Regardless, Harpers Ferry National Historical Park does have an admission fee that must be paid at both parking lots.

Harpers Ferry Train Station Parking Lot
GPS: N 39.324377, W 77.731162

Harpers Ferry National Historical Park Visitor Center
GPS: N 39.316585, W 77.756714

 **TO STOP 1**

Once you arrive in the Lower Town, begin your tour in front of the National Park Service Information Center.

GPS: N 39.322642, W 77.730446

Stop 1 – National Park Service Information Center

Today, the old Master Armorer's house is a good place to get oriented to Harpers Ferry's Lower Town. (kp)

In 1859, the building that now houses the park's Information Center was the Master Armorer's house. The United States Government had completed the structure earlier in 1859, shortly before John Brown's raid. During the raid, the armory's paymaster, John E. P. Daingerfield, lived here. He became a prisoner of Brown's during the raid and did not escape Brown's captivity until the Marines attacked the engine house on the morning of October 18, 1859. Robert E. Lee used the building as his headquarters after he suppressed Brown's raid.

 **To Stop 2**

Facing the Information Center, continue left down Shenandoah Street on the same side of the street as the Information Center. Walk approximately 120 feet until you reach the sign titled "for the deposit of arms" on your right.

GPS: N 39.322883, W 77.730101

Stop 2 – Arsenal Square

The remains of buildings suggest a busy downtown Harpers Ferry in 1859. (kp)

The two Federal arsenal buildings that once stood here stored 100,000 firearms at the time of Brown's raid. Seizing these buildings and the weapons they held was a key part of Brown's plan. Albert Hazlett and Edwin Coppoc initially captured the arsenal but Capt. John Avis's attack on October 17 recaptured parts of Arsenal Square. Raider Dangerfield Newby fell in the street behind you. After Virginia's secession, withdrawing Federal troops burned these two buildings on the night of April 18, 1861.

TO STOP 3

With your back to Shenandoah Street, turn right and quickly turn left onto the gravel path. Follow it as it winds through Arsenal Square until you reach the point where an intersecting path crosses underneath a railroad trestle on your right. Proceed underneath the trestle and continue straight to a set of benches and interpretive markers at The Point.

GPS: N 39.322950, W 77.728539

Stop 3 – The Point

Harpers Ferry's location at the junction of two rivers, the Potomac (left) and the Shenandoah (right), and the Baltimore & Ohio Railroad and Chesapeake & Ohio Canal ensured history would be made at the town. (jeg)

You are standing at the intersection of the Shenandoah (to your right) and Potomac (to your left) rivers. Here, they form the Potomac River, which flows southeast approximately 60 miles downstream past Washington, DC. The empty bridge abutments to your left front are all that remain of the Baltimore & Ohio Railroad Bridge that stood here on the night of October 16, 1859. Brown's raiders crossed the bridge to begin their operations in Harpers Ferry. The Wager House Hotel also stood at The Point as did the B&O Railroad Depot where Heyward Shepherd, the raid's first casualty, died.

TO STOP 4

Turn around and walk several feet, parallel to the Shenandoah River, until you reach a set of steps on your left.

GPS: N 39.322893, W 77.728728

Stop 4 – Gault House Saloon

Nothing remains of the Gault House Saloon that formerly stood at the Point except for the foundation. Militia used the building during the raid. (kp)

The ruins at your feet through which the stairs pass is all that is left of the Gault House Saloon. Militia members fought from and drank from this building along the tracks of the Winchester and Potomac Railroad during Brown's raid.

➡ TO STOP 5

Turn around and again walk underneath the railroad trestle. On your left, just past the gravel path you previously used, is John Brown's Fort.

GPS: N 39.323084, W 77.729517

Stop 5 – John Brown's Fort

John Brown's fort has hopscotched across Harpers Ferry over the years, finally landing near the river overlook. (kp)

The armory's fire engine and guard house, which became John Brown's fort and place of capture on the morning of October 18, 1859, is the original building, though it does not sit in its original location (you will visit that spot at the next stop). It is the only remaining building from the armory. Entrepreneurs purchased the building, dismantled it, and moved it to Chicago for "The World's Columbian Exposition" in 1892-93. It attracted a minimal crowd and subsequently returned to Harpers Ferry. It stood on the Murphy Farm (part of Harpers Ferry National Historical Park) from 1895 to 1909, then on the campus of Storer College from 1909 to 1968. In 1968, the fort came back to Lower Town, close to, but not exactly in, its original location.

➡ **TO STOP 6**

While facing the fort and standing in front of it, turn right. Directly across Shenandoah Street is a staircase. Carefully cross the street and ascend the stairs. At the top is a stone obelisk marking the original site of John Brown's Fort.

GPS: N 39.323472, W 77.729903

Stop 6 – Original Site of John Brown's Fort and the Armory Yard

John Brown's Fort currently sits within view of where it originally stood in 1859. (kp)

The engine house originally stood here but at street level. It was the first building on the left as Brown and his men entered the armory yard. Built in 1848, it now sits approximately 150 feet from its original location. While here, feel free to explore the armory yard, where National Park Service exhibits interpret this archaeological site. To get there, descend another set of steps over your right shoulder as you face the side of the obelisk that reads "John Brown's Fort."

TO STOP 7

Descend the same steps you ascended to reach the building's original location. At the bottom of the steps, immediately turn right and carefully cross Potomac Street. Turn right on the sidewalk and walk approximately fifty feet up Potomac Street to a stone monument on your left.

GPS: N 39.323304, W 77.730053

Stop 7 – Heyward Shepherd Monument

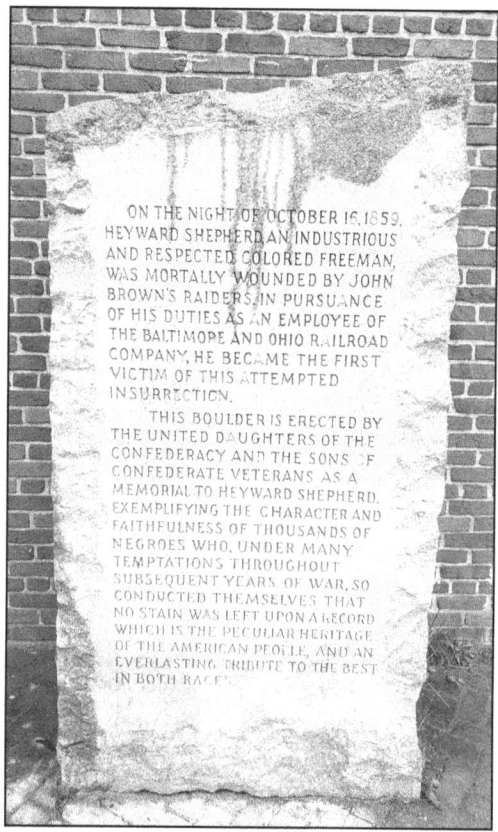

ON THE NIGHT OF OCTOBER 16,1859.
HEYWARD SHEPHERD, AN INDUSTRIOUS
AND RESPECTED COLORED FREEMAN,
WAS MORTALLY WOUNDED BY JOHN
BROWN'S RAIDERS, IN PURSUANCE
OF HIS DUTIES AS AN EMPLOYEE OF
THE BALTIMORE AND OHIO RAILROAD
COMPANY, HE BECAME THE FIRST
VICTIM OF THIS ATTEMPTED
INSURRECTION.

THIS BOULDER IS ERECTED BY
THE UNITED DAUGHTERS OF THE
CONFEDERACY AND THE SONS OF
CONFEDERATE VETERANS AS A
MEMORIAL TO HEYWARD SHEPHERD,
EXEMPLIFYING THE CHARACTER AND
FAITHFULNESS OF THOUSANDS OF
NEGROES WHO, UNDER MANY
TEMPTATIONS THROUGHOUT
SUBSEQUENT YEARS OF WAR, SO
CONDUCTED THEMSELVES THAT
NO STAIN WAS LEFT UPON A RECORD
WHICH IS THE PECULIAR HERITAGE
OF THE AMERICAN PEOPLE, AND AN
EVERLASTING TRIBUTE TO THE BEST
IN BOTH RACES.

This controversial monument commemorates Heyward Shepherd, the first casualty of Brown's Raid and, ironically, a free black man. (kp)

The United Daughters of the Confederacy erected this monument to Heyward Shepherd, whom they claimed exemplified "the character and faithfulness of thousands of negros" when he became the first casualty of Brown's raid. Several hundred people gathered to witness the UDC and the Sons of Confederate Veterans dedicate this monument on October 10, 1931. Originally dubbed the "Faithful Slave Memorial," the monument has created debate from the start. It has also been displayed and removed several times, being placed in storage from 1976-1980 and then covered in plywood until 1995. Several attempts have been made to contextualize the monument. Today, a National Park Service interpretive wayside provides an opposing view of Shepherd's death.

TO STOP 8

Continue down Potomac Street for approximately 600 feet. The monument dedicated to Luke Quinn sits at the base of a long wooden staircase on your left.

GPS: N 39.324299, W 77.731684

Stop 8 – Luke Quinn Monument

Local citizens dedicated this monument to Luke Quinn in 2011. It stands across Potomac Street from the train station. Quinn is buried in St. Peter's Cemetery west of the lower town. (kp)

A local veterans organization raised the money to erect this monument to Pvt. Luke Quinn while a local resident donated the land where it stands. The group dedicated the monument to the only Marine killed in action in Brown's Harpers Ferry Raid in 2011. It should be noted that, despite the monument's text, Quinn was born in Ireland in 1835. He and his family immigrated to the United States in 1844 and he joined the Marine Corps for a four-year enlistment in November 1855. He died just shy of the end of his term.

Hog Alley looks innocuous today, although it has a grisly history. (kp)

TO STOP 9

Proceed down Potomac Street from the direction you just walked. Turn right onto Hog Alley, named so because this is supposedly the location where hogs rooted through Dangerfield Newby's remains. Turn left onto High Street and walk to its intersection with Shenandoah Street. Arsenal square should be across Shenandoah Street from you.

GPS: N 39.322986, W 77.730256

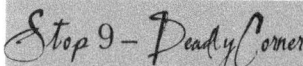

Stop 9 – Deadly Corner

Standing on the "deadly corner," one can look across the street at Arsenal Square. (kp)

Near or at this intersection fell Dangerfield Newby (in front of the arsenal gate), Irish storekeeper Thomas Boerly, and West Point graduate George W. Turner.

 **TO STOP 10**

Turn left on Shenandoah Street until you reach the entrance to the National Park Service's John Brown Museum on your left. Enter the exhibit. Admission is included in your park entrance fee.

GPS: N 39.323122, W 77.730042

Stop 10 – John Brown Museum

This cluster of buildings that witnessed Brown's Raid today house the National Park Service's John Brown Museum. It was also from an upper story window of this row of buildings that the shot was fired that killed Dangerfield Newby. (kp)

This museum details the life of John Brown, focusing especially on his raid here in Harpers Ferry. Three movies are included in the museum, which also displays numerous artifacts related to John Brown's Raid, including an original section of armory fence, the Sharps carbine that Brown wielded during the raid, and more.

This concludes the walking tour of the Lower Town of Harpers Ferry.

For more information on Civil War Trails,
visit www.civilwartrails.org.

Driving Tour of Outlying Raid Sites

APPENDIX B

This driving tour will highlight several sites associated with John Brown's Raid outside Lower Town Harpers Ferry. Several of these sites are part of the popular Civil War Trails program, sporting their distinctive road signs and wayside markers.

Due to the distance between several of these sites, it would not be possible to undertake this tour in chronological order. The tour will necessitate backtracking past the starting point (Harpers Ferry National Park Visitors Center) and runs approximately 30 miles, with sites in both Maryland and West Virginia.

In some instances, this tour will pass historic properties that are privately owned. Please respect the owners' privacy; do not trespass. Other sites include active cemeteries and places of worship; please be respectful of your surroundings.

This tour follows both historic and modern routes. Some are rural and others, particularly Route 340 (William L. Wilson Freeway), may at times have heavy traffic. Other sites are now in neighborhoods and residential areas. Please follow posted speed limits, park only in areas that are both safe and legal, and leave only your footprints behind. Take your time and enjoy all that these locations have to offer.

As John Brown traveled from the jailhouse to the site of his hanging, he remarked to his jailor, John Avis, *"What a beautiful country you have here."* While development has crowded the Harpers Ferry—Charlestown corridor, much of the rolling pastoral beauty that Brown might have recognized in 1859 remains. We hope that you will consider future opportunities to preserve the historical nature of this area.

Enjoy the tour!

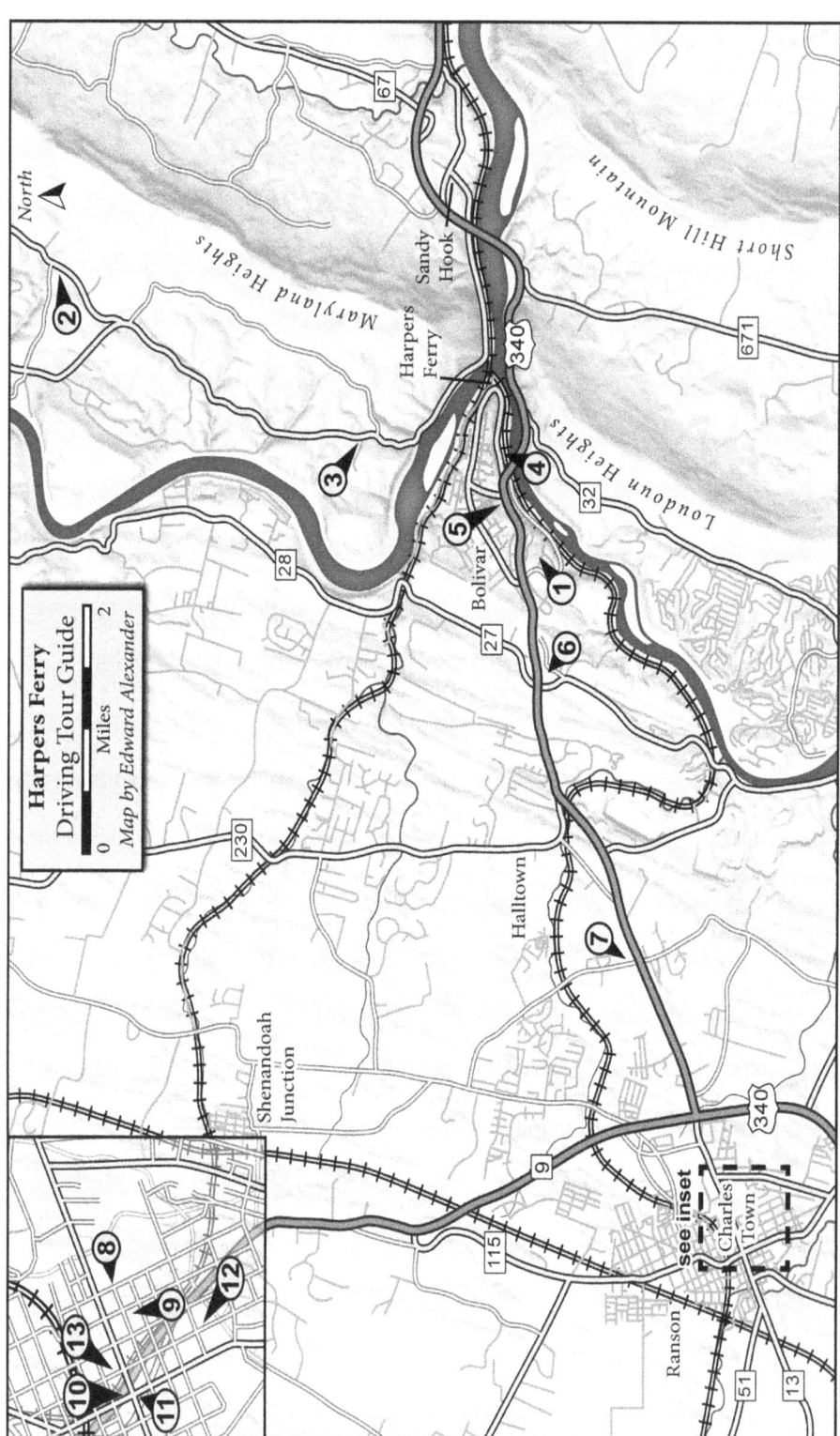

**Harpers Ferry
Driving Tour Guide**

Miles

0   2

Map by Edward Alexander

Stop 1 – Harpers Ferry National Park Visitor Center

Harpers Ferry Visitor Center. (gb)

The John Brown's Raid Driving Tour begins at the Harpers Ferry National Historical Park Visitor Center at Cavalier Heights. The Visitor Center offers a convenient starting point for exploring the multifaceted history of Harpers Ferry. Restroom facilities and parking are available, as well as shuttle service to the Lower Town, where sites associated with the Raid may be visited with the walking tour. Please note the park does charge a per-vehicle entrance fee, payable upon entry.

GPS: N 39.316805, W 77.756942

TO STOP 2

Exit the Visitor Center lot and continue 0.3 miles on Shoreline Drive to the intersection with US Route 340 (William L. Wilson Freeway). Use the right lane to turn right onto Route 340. Use caution as the two lanes quickly merge into one. Follow Route 340 for 3.4 miles, passing through Virginia and into Maryland. After crossing the Sandy Hook Bridge, exit right onto Keep Tryst Road. Follow Keep Tryst Road for 0.2 miles and turn right onto Sandy Hook Road. Follow this road 5.6 miles (after 1.6 miles the name changes to Harpers Ferry Road) and at the Y intersection bear right onto Chestnut Grove Road. Follow it for 0.6 miles to the Kennedy farmhouse on your left. Pull into the driveway. A Civil War Trails sign is located at the end of the fence. A state historical highway marker is located at the entrance to the drive.

GPS: N 39.380096, W 77.715159

Stop 2 – Kennedy Farmhouse

Civil War Trails interprets Brown's stay at the Kennedy farmhouse, as well as Jubal Early's 1864 invasion, which passed by the farmhouse. (jeg)

The Kennedy farmhouse was first built ca. 1840 and was later purchased and renovated by local physician Booth Kennedy. John Brown rented the modest farmhouse from Kennedy's heirs in July 1859 to serve as a headquarters prior to the raid. Here, Brown and his men spent three months finalizing plans for the raid on Harpers Ferry (detailed in Chapter 3 of this book). Brown's men passed much of that time secluded in the attic, protected from the eyes of prying neighbors by Brown's young daughter, Annie. It was from this house on October 16, 1859 that Brown instructed his men to "get on your arms," setting off the cataclysmic event preceding the Civil War.

The property was later purchased by the Improved Benevolent Protective Order of the Elks of the World (the Black Elks), who in the 1950s constructed an auditorium (visible in the treeline behind the farmhouse) that became a popular stop on the famed "Chitlin' Circuit," hosting James Brown, Ray Charles, Aretha Franklin, Marvin Gaye, and other luminaries. The farmhouse was purchased by South Lynn in 1973 and restored to its 1859 appearance, receiving National Historic Landmark status the following year.

The farmhouse is today owned and operated by the John Brown Historical Foundation and is open for tours by appointment only.

To Stop 3

Turn right onto Chestnut Grove Road, traveling 0.6 miles to the stop sign. Make a slight left at the sign and then keep right at the Y to continue onto Harpers Ferry Road. Continue 2.6 miles and turn right into the parking lot at the Pleasantville First Church of God Fellowship Hall.

GPS: N 39.340256, W 77.737795

Stop 3 – Schoolhouse Site

The present church and meeting hall marks the approximate location of the schoolhouse used by Brown's men as a forward armory between Harpers Ferry and the Kennedy farmhouse. (jeg)

Near here stood the one-room country schoolhouse occupied by Brown's men on the morning of October 17. When the raiders appropriated the schoolhouse for their purposes, they found schoolmaster Lind Currie and some thirty students. The schoolhouse served as a forward arsenal for weapons transported from the Kennedy farmhouse by Charles Tidd, William Leeman, and five liberated slaves, under the direction of John Cook. It had been Brown's plan to gather weapons from the schoolhouse before retreating into the mountains.

Currie asked Cook the meaning of the gunfire heard drifting from Harpers Ferry. Cook confidently replied, "Well, it simply means this: that those people down there are resisting our men, and we are shooting them down." United States Marines searched the schoolhouse on October 19 and found sixteen crates of arms and equipment.

The Pleasantville First Church of God was erected in 1888 using materials disassembled from an earlier building along the Chesapeake & Ohio Canal.

To Stop 4

Continue 3.1 miles on Harpers Ferry Road (after 1.5 miles the name changes to Sandy Hook Road). Turn left onto Keep Tryst Road and proceed 0.2 miles (Keep Tryst becomes Valley Road). At the stop sign turn left onto US Route 340 (William L. Wilson Freeway)—use caution in turning as this area sees heavy congestion. Continue 2.7 miles, passing through Virginia and into West Virginia. After crossing the John Hancock Hall Memorial Bridge, make an immediate right onto Shenandoah Street. Continue 0.2 miles to the pull off area on your right.

GPS: N 39.322302, W 77.740181

Stop 4 – United States Rifle Factory

The factory ruins seen along Shoreline Drive stand near the location of Hall's Rifle Works. (jeg)

The United States Rifle Factory on Lower Hall's Island once sat across the Shenandoah Canal to your right. Here, Maine gunsmith John H. Hall perfected precision, uniformity, and interchangeable parts in his patent breechloading rifles, helping to usher in the Industrial Revolution. Hall produced weapons here from 1819–1843. The site then transitioned to the manufacturing arm of the United States Armory at Harpers Ferry and was improved with uniform brick buildings, shops, and a furnace. At the time of John Brown's Raid, the complex included at least eight buildings.

Three of Brown's raiders—John Kagi, John Copeland and Lewis Leary—were stationed at the rifle factory during the raid. On the afternoon of October 17, the three attempted to escape across the Shenandoah River, where Kagi and Leary were both killed and Copeland was captured.

The complex was destroyed in April 1861 at the outbreak of the Civil War. The ruins were visible until removed in 1887 during construction of the Shenandoah Pulp Company. Only the footprints of the buildings remain today.

 ## TO STOP 5

Return to your car and exit the parking lot carefully making a U-turn onto Shenandoah Street. Proceed 300 feet to the stop sign and turn right onto U.S. Route 340 (William L. Wilson Freeway). Continue 0.2 miles, passing Union Street and making a right turn into St. Peter's Cemetery. Bear left on entering the cemetery and continue into the roundabout.

GPS: N 39.320856, W 77.748187

Stop 5 – Luke Quinn Gravesite

Luke Quinn rested in an unmarked grave until 1940. In 2009, a Marine Corps League detachment re-dedicated the grave with a flagpole and marker. (jeg)

You are now in the burial grounds of St. Peter's Catholic Church, which was founded in Harpers Ferry in 1831 to serve the growing number of Catholics in the region. Two figures who featured prominently in John Brown's Raid are buried here. Reverend Michael Costello (Gravesite GPS: N 39.321724, W 77.748825) was pastor during the raid and wrote a detailed account of his experiences. Costello imparted the last rites to civilian casualty Thomas Boerly and the lone United States Marine killed in action, Pvt. Luke Quinn. Costello also visited Brown in Charlestown before his execution. During the Civil War, Costello flew the British Union Jack flag atop the church in an effort to preserve the edifice from destruction. Costello died in 1867 and is buried here, his plot encircled by an iron fence near the top of the hill.

Just down the hill from Costello is the grave of Pvt. Luke Quinn (Gravesite GPS: N 39.321340, W 77.748619), who fell mortally wounded in the final attack on the engine house. Quinn's remains were first excavated in 1927 and laid in an unmarked grave until 1940. A new marker and flagpole were installed in 2012. Quinn is also memorialized with a monument on Potomac Street in Harpers Ferry.

 ## To Stop 6

Return to your car and proceed to the cemetery entrance. Exit right onto U.S. Route 340 (William L. Wilson Freeway). Continue 1.5 miles. At the traffic light use the left lane to turn left onto Millville Road. Continue 0.3 miles and turn left onto Allstadts Hill Road. Continue 0.2 miles to Allstadt's Ordinary on your left. Park in the gravel drive. A Civil War Trails marker is located to your left.

GPS: N 39.315806, W 77.772288

Stop 6 – Allstadt's Corner

Constructed circa 1790, the property was later purchased by Jacob Allstadt, who operated an Ordinary (tavern) and a nearby tollhouse on the Harpers Ferry–Charlestown Turnpike. At the time of John Brown's Raid, Jacob's son, John Hall Allstadt, lived here with his family. Early on the morning of October 17, a detachment of Brown's men under Capt. John E. Cook arrived at the house, taking John Allstadt, his son John Thomas, and seven slaves hostage. They were conveyed to the engine house in Harpers Ferry and survived the raid unharmed. John

The Allstadt house was built on 1,675 acres that belonged to the Lee family, one of the "First Families of Virginia." (jeg)

Thomas Allstadt briefly served in the Stonewall Brigade during the Civil War, and, according to his headstone (Edge Hill Cemetery, Charles Town), was the last surviving hostage of John Brown's Raid at the time of his death in 1923.

The Allstadt property also saw action during the September 1862 Battle of Harpers Ferry. Known today as Allstadt's Corner, this property was preserved by the American Battlefield Trust and in 2019 was transferred to Harpers Ferry National Historical Park.

   ## TO STOP 7

Return to your car and proceed 0.2 miles back down Allstadt's Hill Road, turning right onto Millville Road. Continue 0.3 miles to the traffic light at U.S. Route 340 (William L. Wilson Freeway). Turn left onto U.S. Route 340 and continue 2.5 miles. Use the right lane to turn right onto Old Country Club Road. Continue 0.1 miles to the state highway historical sign on your right. Use the shoulder area to park.

GPS: N 39.305000, W 77.816532

Stop 7 – Beall-Air House

Approximately one mile ahead is Beall-Air, the circa 1820 estate owned by Colonel Lewis Washington, a great-grandnephew of George Washington. During John

Beall-Air, constructed in 1820, still stands in a housing community that bears its name. (kp)

Brown's Raid, a detachment of Brown's men under the command of Capt. John E. Cook used a fence rail to break down the back door and take Col. Washington hostage. Cook befriended Washington weeks earlier, and even visited Beall-Air. During one of his visits, he and Washington shot targets in the front yard.

The raiders also took from Beall-Air three of Washington's male slaves, a sword presented to George Washington by Frederick the Great, later presented to John Brown, and a pistol presented by the Marquis de Lafayette, retained by Cook. From Beall-Air the raiders next stopped at Allstadt's Corner, before returning to Harpers Ferry.

Beall-Air is today located inside the gated Beallair Community. This site is only accessible via pre-arranged appointment with the community office.

➡ TO STOP 8

Caution: Do not attempt a U-turn from this site, as a blind hill in front of you obstructs traffic from view. Continue 0.2 miles and turn right onto Sleepy Hollow Circle. Bear left and continue for 0.1 miles, turning right onto Fairway Drive. Continue 0.1 miles and turn right onto Sleepy Hollow Circle, continuing 0.1 miles back to the intersection with Old Country Road.

Turn left onto Old Country Road and continue 0.3 miles to the traffic light at the intersection with U.S. Route 340 (William L. Wilson Freeway). Turn right onto U.S. Route 340 and continue 2.3 miles (after 1.5 miles the road becomes WV-51 / E. Washington Street). Turn left onto S. Seminary Street and continue approximately 330 feet to Edge Hill Cemetery on your left. There is no street parking available on S. Seminary Street, so please enter the cemetery gates and park. A Civil War Trails marker is located at the cemetery entrance.

GPS: N 39.289955, W 77.854454

Stop 8 - Edge Hill Cemetery

Founded in 1858, Edge Hill Cemetery is the final resting place for three personalities associated with John Brown's Raid—Fontaine Beckham, John Avis, and John W. Rowan. Beckham (Gravesite GPS: N 39.290094, W. 77.858424) was the mayor of Harpers Ferry and stationmaster of the Baltimore & Ohio Railroad at the

Edge Hill Cemetery is the final resting place of a number of people related to the John Brown story. (kp)

The graves of Fontaine Beckham (left), John Avis (center), and John Rowan (right). (kp)

time of the raid. He was shot and killed by Edwin Coppoc while investigating the commotion near the armory compound. Honoring the wishes outlined in his will, Beckham's slaves were freed after his death—the only slaves freed directly as a result of John Brown's Raid.

Also buried at Edge Hill is John Avis (Gravesite GPS: N 39.290125, W. 77.854244), jailor at the Jefferson County jail in Charlestown. Avis led a company of militia during the raid, though he was also noted for his kindness to Brown during his time as an inmate in Avis's jail. In recognition of his kindness, Brown presented Avis with his silver pocket watch before his execution and kissed Avis's child while departing the jail. Avis's final task for his inmate was placing the noose around Brown's neck on the gallows. He served in the 5th Virginia Infantry (CSA) during the Civil War and died in 1883.

Captain John W. Rowan (Gravesite GPS: N 39.290121, W 77.853427) commanded the Jefferson Guards during John Brown's Raid, securing the Baltimore & Ohio bridge and closing Brown's avenue of escape into Maryland. He commanded Company A, 2nd Virginia Infantry during the Civil War.

To Stop 9

Use the Cemetery Drive to loop back around to the main entrance. Continue straight on E. Washington Street for 500 feet. Zion Episcopal Church will be on your left. There is a roundabout drive inside the gates, though please use street parking for extended visits. A Civil War Trails marker is located just inside the gates.

GPS: N 39.289405, W 77.856000

Stop 9 – Zion Episcopal Church and Cemetery

While the Zion Episcopal Church was founded in 1818, the church building in front of you dates to 1851. Following John Brown's Raid, the church was used to house several companies of Virginia militia detailed to Charlestown for Brown's execution. The church was heavily damaged during the Civil War and later restored.

The cemetery is the final resting place for several persons associated with John Brown's Raid. Colonel Lewis Washington (Gravesite GPS: N 39.288880, W 77.855488) was captured at his Beall-Air estate and confined in the engine house as one of Brown's most prominent prisoners. Washington testified against Brown during his trial, though admitted Brown treated his captives kindly. He served the Confederacy in the Civil War and died in 1871.

John Starry (Gravesite GPS: N 39.288765, W 77.856312) was a physician living in Harpers Ferry at the time of the raid. He treated Hayward Shepherd's mortal wound and later helped raise alarm of the attack in the neighborhood of Harpers Ferry and Charlestown.

Colonel Robert Baylor (Gravesite GPS: N 39.289219, W 77.855768) commanded the Virginia militia at John Brown's Raid and communicated with Brown in attempts to end the hostilities.

George Sadler (Gravesite GPS: N 39.288663, W 77.855874) was a local undertaker who built the coffin for Brown, and was responsible for transporting him to the gallows.

George Turner (Gravesite GPS: N 39.288809, W 77.856020), a graduate of the United States Military Academy at West Point and a friend of Robert E. Lee, owned nearby Wheatland Plantation at the time of John Brown's Raid. Turner was shot and killed by one of Brown's men on October 17, 1859.

The graves of John Starry (top left), Robert Baylor (top center), George Sadler (top right), George Turner (bottom left, and Lawson Botts (bottom center). (kp)

Also buried here is Lawson Botts (Gravesite GPS: N 39.288748, W 77.855741), one of Brown's defense attorneys and later colonel of the 2nd Virginia Infantry (CSA), who was killed at the Battle of Second Manassas in August 1862.

➡ TO STOP 10

Exit the church drive and turn left on E. Congress Street. Continue 0.2 miles, turning right onto S. George Street. Continue 400 feet, passing straight through the traffic light. The Jefferson County Courthouse is on your right. Street parking is available on S. George Street next to the courthouse, E. Washington Street in front of the courthouse and E. Library Street behind the courthouse. A Civil War Trails marker is located near the courthouse entrance. A state highway historical marker for Brown confidant Martin R. Delany is located to the left of the courthouse.

GPS: N 39.289275, W 77.859891

Stop 10 – Jefferson County Courthouse

The courthouse in front of you was built in 1836 and served as a backdrop for the trial of John Brown and six of his men. Brown's trial began on October 27, 1859, and lasted only one week. The jury took only 45 minutes to convict Brown.

The building was heavily damaged during the Civil War and was a focal point of an 1863 attack by Confederate Gen. John D. Imboden. The courthouse was extensively restored in 1872, such that the only surviving room from John Brown's Trial is the Jefferson County Commission room on the first floor of the building.

The building remains a working courthouse. Please be respectful of those conducting business.

 **TO STOP 11**

Follow traffic signals and utilize the crosswalk directly in front of the courthouse to cross WV-51/E. Washington Street. Turn right and utilize the crosswalk to cross S. George Street. The Charles Town Post Office is directly in front of you.

The Jefferson County Courthouse that stands today in Charles Town is the same one that housed Brown's trial, though both its interior and exterior have changed since 1859. (kp)

GPS: N 39.2889877, W 77.8600578

Stop 11 – Jefferson County Jail Site

On this site in front of you stood the former Jefferson County Jail. Here, Brown and his men were confined following the Raid until the time of their execution. Jailer John Avis and his family also utilized the jail as their residence. On the night of December 15, 1859, one night before their execution, John E. Cook and Edwin Coppoc made a failed attempt to escape over the wall in the rear of the jail. The jail was later torn down and the current post office building was erected in 1922.

A plaque on the front of the Charles Town post office denotes the site as the location of the former jail, which sat diagonally across the town's main intersection from the courthouse. (kp)

 **TO STOP 12**

From your position in front of the Post Office, turn left and make an immediate right on S. George Street. Travel 0.3 miles. Turn left onto Hunter Street and continue 400 feet before turning right onto S. Samuel Street. The site of John Brown's execution will be on your immediate left. A parking berm is available just ahead on your right. A Civil War Trails marker and a state highway historical marker are located near the entrance to the property. Please note this home is private property and is not publicly accessible.

GPS: N 39.285851, W 77.856451

The area around you was an open field in 1859. The gallows were constructed here for the execution of John Brown on December 2, 1859. One witness described the area as "a rising ground, and commanded the outstretching valley from mountain to mountain." During the execution, the site was flanked by approximately 1,500 Virginia militiamen and cadets from the Virginia Military Institute.

The site was utilized again just two weeks later for the executions of John E. Cook, John Anthony Copeland, Edwin Coppoc, and Shields Green, and again in March 1860 for the executions of Albert Hazlett and Aaron D. Stevens.

The house on this site was constructed in 1891 by Colonel John T. Gibson, who commanded the 55th Regiment of Virginia Militia during John Brown's Raid, and is today listed on the National Register of Historic Places.

 **TO STOP 13**

Continue south on S. Samuel Street for 0.1 miles and turn left at the first cross street onto Mason Street. Continue 360 feet and turn left at the first intersection onto S. Mildred Street. Continue 0.4 miles and turn left onto E. Washington Street. Continue 110 feet and turn right at the first cross street onto N. Samuel Street. The Jefferson County Museum is on your right. Street parking is available, as well as a small lot between the museum and the neighboring Presbyterian Church. A Civil War Trails marker is located to your right near the museum entrance.

GPS: N 39.289786, W 77.858765

The gallows where Brown and six of his followers were executed rested in a large field outside Charlestown. Today, they would have stood between the photographer's position and the 1891 Gibson-Todd House. John Thomas Gibson, who commanded Virginia militia during the raid, constructed the house. (kp)

Stop 13 – Jefferson County Museum

Since 1965, the Jefferson County Museum has interpreted the rich history of the local area, from the Native Americans who called the area home to the present day. Of particular interest to visitors of this driving tour, the Museum displays the wagon used to transport John Brown from the jailhouse to the gallows, pikes intended for use in arming the slaves, and items from both the jailhouse where Brown was held and the Jefferson County Courthouse where he was tried. The Museum also offers exhibits on slavery in the Jefferson County area, local Civil War history, including arms, ammunition, uniforms and flags, and Storer College and the Niagara Movement.

Please note the museum is open seasonally (mid-March–mid-December) and does charge an admission fee. Please contact the museum prior to your visit to confirm hours and availability.

This concludes the driving tour of John Brown's Raid Sites.

From 1909 to 1968, John Brown's Fort sat on the campus of Storer College above Harpers Ferry. College alumni placed this plaque on the side of the building to commemorate Brown and his raiders. (jm)

Biographies of John Brown's Raiders

APPENDIX C

Jeremiah Goldsmith Anderson was born in Putnam County, Indiana on April 17, 1833, a descendant of Virginia slaveholders. Removing to Kansas in 1857, he was tormented by Missouri border ruffians before joining with Brown. A trusted lieutenant in Brown's Provisional Army, Anderson was mortally wounded by a bayonet thrust which pinned him to the wall during the final assault on the engine house. His body was mutilated before being transferred to nearby Winchester Medical College for dissection. Brown wrote to Anderson's father from his jail cell that his son had been "fighting bravely by my side" before falling.

Osborne Perry Anderson was born to free African American parents in Chester County, Pennsylvania on July 27, 1830. He attended Oberlin College (Ohio) and later moved to Chatham, Canada West, where, in 1858, he met Brown. Anderson was present for the capture of Lewis Washington, receiving the sword of Washington's great uncle, George Washington, which was presented to Brown. Later stationed at the arsenal, Anderson made a successful escape from Harpers Ferry through Pennsylvania and into Canada. In 1861, he published *A Voice From Harper's Ferry*, an eyewitness account of the raid and his escape. He recruited African American soldiers during the Civil War and died in December 1872 at Washington, DC. He is buried at National Harmony Memorial Park in Hyattsville, Maryland.

Oliver Brown was born on March 9, 1839, at Franklin Mills, Ohio, the youngest son of John and Mary Ann Brown to live to adulthood. He traveled with his father to Kansas and North Elba, where he married Martha Brewster in April 1858. His pregnant wife joined him the following year at the Kennedy farmhouse. Though he expressed his doubts to his father regarding the attack on Harpers Ferry, Oliver was an active participant in the raid, guarding the B&O railroad bridge before being mortally wounded inside the engine house on the afternoon of October 17. His body remained buried near the Shenandoah River until being exhumed in 1899 and reburied next to his father at North Elba. Born several months after Oliver's death, his daughter lived only two days and his wife died one month later.

Owen Brown, the third son of John and Dianthe Brown, was born on November 4, 1824. While a childhood injury crippled one arm, Owen served with his father in Kansas and Virginia. His wife joined him at the Kennedy farmhouse where, like his brother Oliver, he expressed dissatisfaction with his father's plan of attack. He was ultimately detailed as a rear guard at the farmhouse, instructed to deliver the guns and pikes when called. Escaping through Pennsylvania, Owen avoided capture, moving to Ohio and eventually settling in Pasadena, California, where he died on January 8, 1889, the last surviving member of his father's Provisional Army. He is buried on private property in Altadena, California.

Watson Brown was born on October 7, 1835, the second child born to his father's second wife, Mary Ann. He tended to the farm in North Elba while his father and brothers were in Kansas, though he joined them at the Kennedy farmhouse in August 1859. Watson was shot by the angry mob while negotiating a ceasefire. He was able to drag himself back to the engine house, lingering in pain until his death on October 19. When asked about his participation in the attack, Brown said "I did my duty as I saw it." His body was transferred to Winchester Medical College and was recovered in 1862 by a Union surgeon who sent the remains to Indiana, where they remained until positively identified by John Brown Jr. in 1882, when they were reburied at North Elba.

John Edwin Cook was born on May 12, 1829, in Haddam, Connecticut. He moved to Kansas in late 1855 and joined Brown the following year. Brown appointed Cook as his agent in Harpers Ferry; Cook arrived there in June 1858 to scout the area and its inhabitants. He married and fathered a son before Brown and the provisional army arrived the following summer. Named a Captain, Cook led the raiders to capture Lewis Washington and John Allstadt before returning to Maryland to gather weapons. He escaped to Chambersburg but was captured there on October 26. Removed to Charlestown, he penned a lengthy jailhouse confession but was sentenced to death. An appeal for a pardon on behalf of Cook's brother-in-law, then Governor of Indiana, failed. He was executed on December 16, 1859, and is buried at Greenwood Cemetery in Brooklyn.

John Anthony Copeland was born on August 15, 1834, at Raleigh, North Carolina. His family moved to Ohio, where he attended Oberlin College and became involved in anti-slavery activities, including participating in the famed Oberlin-Wellington Rescue of 1858. He and his uncle, Lewis Leary, joined Brown's provisional army in the summer of 1859 and arrived at the Kennedy farm that September. Stationed at the rifle works on Hall's Island during the raid, Copeland was captured in the Shenandoah River and imprisoned in the jail at Charlestown, where he was executed on December 16, 1859. His body was taken to Winchester Medical College and was never recovered.

Barclay Coppoc was born on January 4, 1839, in Columbiana County, Ohio. His Quaker family moved to Springdale, Iowa in 1850, where he and his older brother Edwin first met Brown and later joined the provisional army. Suffering from consumption, Barclay was stationed at the Kennedy farmhouse during the raid, escaping from there to Chambersburg on a route that would take him as far as Canada before he arrived back in Iowa in 1860. Avoiding a bounty for his arrest, Coppoc was commissioned a 1st Lieutenant in the 3rd Kansas Infantry during the Civil War. He was mortally wounded in a train wreck at Platte River Bridge, Missouri on September 3, 1861. He died the next day and is buried in Leavenworth, Kansas.

Edwin Coppoc was born on June 30, 1835, and, with his brother, joined Brown's provisional army in 1858, where he was commissioned a lieutenant. Coppoc was stationed at the arsenal building during the raid before removing to the engine house, from which point he shot and killed Harpers Ferry's mayor Fontaine Beckham. Captured during the final attack on the engine house, Coppoc was jailed at Charlestown. An escape attempt with fellow prisoner Cook failed, and both were executed on December 16, 1859. In a letter written shortly before his execution, Coppoc predicted that "by the taking of my life, and the lives of my comrades, Virginia is but hastening . . . when the slave shall rejoice in his freedom." His body was returned to Salem, Ohio, for burial.

Shields Green, also known as Esau Brown or simply "Emperor," was born a slave in Charleston, South Carolina, circa 1836. Fleeing to Rochester, New York, Green befriended Frederick Douglass, who in turn introduced him to John Brown. Green joined Brown at Chambersburg, Pennsylvania, in August 1859. Douglass recalled that Green preferred to "go wid de ol' man." He was present for the capture of Lewis Washington and John Allstadt and guarded prisoners inside the engine house, where he was captured during the final attack. Jailed in Charlestown, Green was executed on December 16, 1859. His body was taken to Winchester Medical College and was never recovered.

Albert Hazlett was born on September 21, 1837, in Pennsylvania. Later removing to Kansas, Hazlett joined John Brown in late 1858. Stationed at the arsenal during the raid, he and raider Osborne Anderson escaped across the Potomac River and into Maryland. While Anderson made good on his escape, Hazlett was captured in Cumberland County, Pennsylvania and jailed at Charlestown. Hazlett maintained his innocence, claiming his name was "William Harrison," but was nonetheless convicted and executed on March 16, 1860. First buried in New Jersey, Hazlett was disinterred in 1899 and reburied with John Brown and his comrades at North Elba.

John Henri Kagi was born on March 15, 1835, in Bristolville, Ohio. He moved to Nebraska in 1855 and then to Kansas, where he joined the Free-State Volunteers (under command of fellow raider Aaron Stevens) and was an active participant in Bleeding Kansas. Kagi joined John Brown in 1857 and was later named "Secretary of War" in Brown's provisional government. Stationed at the rifle works on Hall's Island during the raid, he unsuccessfully pleaded with Brown to disengage and retreat back into Maryland. He was shot and killed while fleeing across the Shenandoah River. His body remained buried along the banks of the river until 1899 when he was disinterred and reburied next to John Brown at North Elba.

Lewis Sheridan Leary was born on March 17, 1835, in Fayetteville, North Carolina. Born to free African American parents, Leary moved to Oberlin, Ohio, where he was active in anti-slavery activities and participated in the Oberlin-Wellington Rescue in 1858. Stationed at the rifle works during the raid on Harpers Ferry, Leary was mortally wounded while attempting to cross the Shenandoah River. Pulled back to shore, he suffered for more than eight hours before expiring from his wounds. He was buried in a mass grave near the river and in 1899 was reinterred at North Elba. His widow remarried in 1869–a daughter born of that second marriage gave birth to a son, acclaimed poet Langston Hughes.

William Henry Leeman was born on March 20, 1839, in Hallowell, Maine, and was the youngest of Brown's raiders. Joining Brown in Kansas in the fall of 1856, he proclaimed slavery to be "the greatest curse that ever infested America." Commissioned a Captain in Brown's army, Leeman was sent back to the farmhouse during the raid to retrieve more weapons, returning to the engine house with an additional prisoner. While attempting to surrender in the middle of the Potomac River, Leeman was shot at point blank range and killed by a resident of Bolivar. His body was used for target practice before being buried in a mass grave near the Shenandoah River. His body was reinterred at North Elba in 1899.

Francis Jackson Meriam was born on November 17, 1837, in Framingham, Massachusetts. Born to a wealthy abolitionist family, Meriam was considered frail and was blind in one eye, but joined Brown at the Kennedy farmhouse in the days leading up to the raid, where he was detailed to remain and guard weapons. He escaped from the farmhouse and made it as far as Canada to successfully evade capture for his part in the raid. During the Civil War, Meriam served as a captain in the 3rd South Carolina Infantry and later in the 59th and 57th Massachusetts Infantry and was wounded at the Battle of Spotsylvania in May 1864. Meriam died in New York City on November 28, 1865.

Dangerfield Newby was born circa 1820 in Fauquier County, Virginia, the oldest son of a slave mother and a white father. In late 1858, his parents relocated the family to eastern Ohio, forcing Dangerfield to leave his enslaved wife and children in Virginia. His wife wrote Dangerfield, begging him to purchase their freedom. After unsuccessful negotiations with her owner, Dangerfield joined John Brown's army in 1859, intending to liberate his family by force. Newby was the first of the raiders to fall, pierced through the neck by an iron spike near the arsenal gate. His body was mutilated by townspeople and hogs. He was buried in the mass grave along the Shenandoah River and reburied at North Elba in 1899.

Aaron Dwight Stevens was born on March 15, 1831, in Lisbon, Connecticut. After serving in the Mexican War, Stevens was imprisoned in Kansas before escaping and joining John Brown. He was an active participant in Bleeding Kansas. As second in command of Brown's army and his most trusted subordinate, Stevens was shot and captured while conveying a flag of truce from the engine house. Thought to be mortally wounded, Stevens survived and was jailed at Charlestown, writing to Brown's family from his jail cell that "some of us must suffer that the rest may learn." He was executed on March 16, 1860, and was first buried in New Jersey and later disinterred in 1899 and reburied at North Elba.

Stewart Taylor was born on October 29, 1836, at Uxbridge, Canada. Later relocating to Iowa, he joined John Brown in 1858 and arrived at the Kennedy farmhouse two months before the raid. Though not born in the United States, Taylor was described as "heart and soul in the anti-slavery cause." He was detailed to guard the B&O Railroad Bridge, later retreating to the armory and finally the engine house. Taylor spoke of a premonition of his death at Harpers Ferry, which was realized when he was mortally wounded inside the door of the engine house. He was buried in the mass grave along the Shenandoah River and was reinterred at North Elba in 1899.

Dauphin Osgood Thompson was born on April 17, 1838 at North Elba, New York. The Thompsons were neighbors of the Brown family at North Elba; two of the Thompson children married two of Brown's children. Dauphin arrived at the Kennedy farmhouse with his older brother William and brother-in-law Watson Brown in August 1859. Writing from the farmhouse that fall, he boasted to his family that pro-slavery advocates "will find out we know what we are about." Commissioned as a lieutenant in Brown's army, Thompson was bayoneted and killed during the final assault on the engine house. He was buried in the mass grave along the Shenandoah River and was reinterred at North Elba in 1899.

William Thompson was born in New Hampshire in August 1833. He attempted to join John Brown in Kansas in 1856 but returned to his home in North Elba after meeting Brown's sons on their return trip from Kansas. He arrived at the Kennedy farmhouse in August 1859 and was detailed to guard the Baltimore & Ohio Railroad Bridge during the early stages of the raid. Later forced into the engine house, Thompson and a prisoner were sent under a flag of truce to negotiate a ceasefire. He was grabbed and conducted to the Gault House Saloon, from which point he was dragged to the banks of the Potomac River and executed. His body was thrown in the river and used as target practice for the remainder of the raid. He was buried with his brother Dauphin and the other raiders in the mass grave along the Shenandoah River and was reinterred with them at North Elba in 1899.

Charles Plummer Tidd was born in Palermo, Maine, in 1834. He relocated to Kansas in 1856 and joined John Brown the following year, becoming one of his most trusted associates and later a captain in Brown's provisional army. Tidd objected to Brown's plans at Harpers Ferry, going so far as to leave the Kennedy farmhouse for a time to reevaluate his own plans. He eventually returned to the farmhouse and participated in the raid, in which Brown detailed him to gather additional weapons in Maryland. He escaped as far as Canada before returning to Massachusetts, where he enlisted in the 21st Massachusetts Infantry. He died of fever near Roanoke Island, North Carolina on February 7, 1862, and is buried at the New Bern National Cemetery.

All images of the raiders in this section were provided by West Virginia Archives & History.

Suggested Reading
JOHN BROWN'S RAID

The Zealot and the Emancipator: John Brown, Abraham Lincoln, and the Struggle for American Freedom
H. W. Brands
Doubleday, 2020
ISBN-13: 978-0385544009

Bestselling author H. W. Brands's dual biography of John Brown and Abraham Lincoln examines both men's lifelong views of slavery and how both played radically different roles in achieving the same end: the abolition of slavery.

Freedom's Dawn: The Last Days of John Brown in Virginia
Louis DeCaro Jr.
Rowman & Littlefield, 2015
ISBN-13: 978-1442236721

An exhaustive account of John Brown's time in Virginia, from the end of the raid, through the trial and confinement, to the gallows and destiny.

Confluence: Harpers Ferry as Destiny
Dennis E. Frye and Catherine Mägi Oliver
Harpers Ferry Park Association, 2019
ISBN-13: 978-0967403359

An all-encompassing history of Harpers Ferry, including John Brown's Raid, what brought him to Harpers Ferry, and what ultimately doomed his campaign.

Midnight Rising: John Brown and the Raid That Sparked the Civil War
Tony Horwitz
Henry Holt & Company, 2011
ISBN-13: 978-0805091533

A masterful narrative history of John Brown's Raid from the acclaimed author of *Confederates in the Attic*.

To Purge This Land with Blood: A Biography of John Brown
Stephen B. Oates
University of Massachusetts Press, 1984
ISBN-13: 978-0870234583

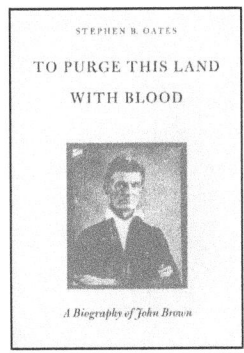

First published fifty years ago, Oates's definitive biography of John Brown has held up well, tracing Brown's life from childhood to the grave.

The Secret Six: The True Tale of the Men Who Conspired with John Brown
Edward J. Renehan, Jr.
Crown Publishers, Inc., 1995
ISBN: 051759028X

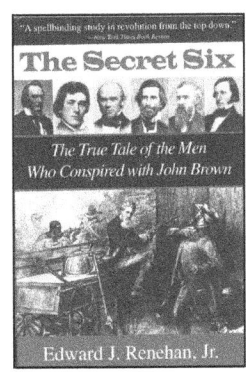

This book outlines the lives of John Brown's financiers, their ties to Brown, and how the raid shaped both their lives and memory.

John Brown, Abolitionist: The Man Who Killed Slavery, Sparked the Civil War, and Seeded Civil Rights
David S. Reynolds
Vintage, 2006
ISBN-13: 978-0375726156

Reynolds's treatment of Brown is not just a biography but also an attempt to place Brown, his motives, and his actions in the context of the mid-nineteenth century. The book also measures Brown against other freedom fighters throughout history.

About the Authors

Jon-Erik M. Gilot has worked more than fifteen years in the field of public history. In addition to his work as a business archivist and records manager, he also serves as curator at the Captain Thomas Espy Grand Army of the Republic Post in Carnegie, Pennsylvania, and is active in numerous historical organizations. This is his first book.

Kevin R. Pawlak is a historic site manager for the Prince William County Office of Historic Preservation. He also is a certified battlefield guide at Antietam National Battlefield, Harpers Ferry National Historical Park, and South Mountain Battlefield. Kevin is on the board of directors of the Save Historic Antietam Foundation and the Antietam Institute. He previously worked as an interpretive ranger at Harpers Ferry National Historical Park. This is his fifth book.